The Book of Honey

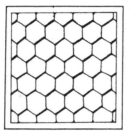

Honey is the epic of love
The materialization of the infinite
The soul and the blood of flowers
Condensed through the spirit of others

—Garcia Lorca

The Book of Honey

Claude Francis &
Fernande Gontier

Illustrated by Stephen Zinkus

AUTUMN ❁ PRESS

Published by Autumn Press, Inc.
with editorial offices at
25 Dwight Street
Brookline, Massachusetts 02146
Distributed in the United States
by Random House, Inc., and in
Canada by Random House of Canada, Ltd.

Library of Congress Catalog Card Number: 78-73469
ISBN: 0-394-73775-X
Printed in the United States of America
Typeset at dnh, Cambridge, Massachusetts
Book design and typography by Beverly Stiskin

Table of Contents

The bee is more honored than other animals,
not because she labors, but because she labors for others.
—St. John Chrysostom, *Homilies*

Preface

This is a practical book for people who want to know how to select and use honey in their daily diet. Usually, when someone decides to turn to natural foods, the first thing he or she does is to replace sugar with honey. Like so many people, we did just that, but we wanted to know if we had good reason to do so. Once we began to ask questions, one thing led to another. We started to accumulate facts, we visited beekeepers, we interviewed honey merchants, we talked with people who used honey, and we read. We found out that there are many misconceptions about honey and that a book about honey cookery, geared for the neophyte, might be very useful.

Honeylore is as fascinating as it is inexhaustible. Very few basic products enjoy such universal popularity. Today the consumption of raw, natural honey is growing as people become aware of its nutritional value: it has all the vitamins, minerals, and enzymes necessary for the metabolism of its sugars, and all the elements needed for the maintenance of animal tissue. Unlike sugar, which is pure sweetness and empty calories,[1] raw, unprocessed honey is a concentrated store of potential energy and life.

Like most people, we started out knowing very little about the many possible uses of honey; we were familiar with it only as a sweet spread for bread, pancakes, or toast, and then as a sweetener for coffee or tea. Through our research, however, we learned that honey has long

---

1. Refined or processed sugars lack the trace elements needed for metabolism. In his testimony to the Senate Subcommittee on Environmental Pollution in 1970, Dr. Schroeder, Director of the Trace Element Laboratory at Dartmouth Medical School, quoted a study on the refining of raw sugar into white sugar, showing that refining removes 93 percent of the ash which is essential for metabolism of the sugar, 61 percent of the manganese, 92 percent of the cobalt, 76 percent of the copper, 67 percent of the zinc, and most of the chromium and magnesium.

been used in various cultures not only in pastries and desserts, but also in cooking meat, fowl, fish, and vegetables.

In the Provence region of France where we grew up, honey is still an important part of old folk traditions, and recipes involving honey are very much alive today. On Christmas Day, for example, thirteen desserts are traditionally served, one of which is honey; another is nougat honey candy. One of the most famous French honey candies, *le calisson,* came from the kitchens of King René, a gourmet, poet, and patron of the arts who lived in Aix-en-Provence in the fourteenth century. To this day, the recipe is kept secret and transmitted from generation to generation in the same family.

We tried some of the traditional recipes that we researched, but, finding most of them too complicated for everyday cooking, decided to adapt them to our own needs. Cooking with honey, we learned, can be very creative and very rewarding.

A thousand honey secrets shalt thou know.
—Shakespeare

What Is Honey?

Composition

Honey is the nectar and saccharine exudations of plants that are gathered, modified, and stored in honeycombs by honeybees.

Nectar is composed of water which the plants draw from the soil. As it travels up the stems, this water carries with it sugars, minerals, vitamins, and a number of other substances which differ from plant to plant. The bees gather the nectar from the flowers, condense it, and transform it through the chemistry of their own bodies.

The various honeys have different tastes, colors, textures, and properties, depending on the plants, the nature of the soil, the weather patterns, the climate, and the season of the harvest, so that no two honeys are alike (see Table 1). Basically, however all honey is composed of two simple sugars: glucose and levulose (the latter is also called fructose). The body is able to assimilate these sugars just as they are because the bees have already accomplished the necessary inversion into simple sugars, thus sparing the human gastrointestinal tract. Glucose is absorbed directly into the blood, and fructose somewhat less rapidly. Since no chemical changes are necessary, honey is a source of quick energy.

Honey contains all the vitamins that nutritionists consider necessary for health; it contains the B vitamins, thiamine, riboflavin, niacin, pantothenic acid, pyridoxine, and biotin, as well as ascorbic acid (vitamin C) and nicotinic acid. All these vitamins play a vital role in human nutrition. And unlike fruits and vegetables which lose some of their vitamin content during harvesting, storage, and preparation, honey—unless it is overheated—never loses its vitamins.

Honey also contains all the trace minerals that are essential to health: iron, copper, manganese, silice, chlorine, calcium, potassium, sodium, phosphorus, aluminum, and magnesium. The mineral content of each variety of honey differs according to the mineral resources in the

9

Table 1. Origin of Floral Types

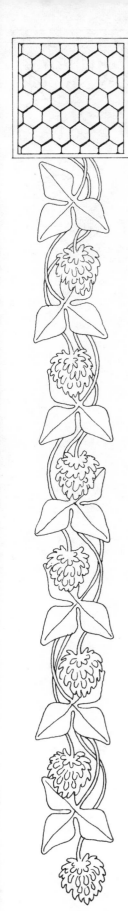

Alabama:
Sweetclover.
Tuliptree.
Rattan.
Cotton.
Blackberry.
White clover.

Arizona:
Mesquite.
Arrowweed.
Catclaw.
Alfalfa.
Tamarisk.
Sweetclover.

Arkansas:
White clover.
Persimmon.
Spanish-needles.

California:
Sage.
Alfalfa.
Orange.
Wild buckwheat.
Star-thistle.
Mustard.
Lima bean.
Manzanita.

Colorado:
Sweetclover.
Alfalfa.
Cleome.
White clover.
Rosinweed.
Alsike clover.
Sunflower.

Connecticut:
Sweetclover.
White clover.
Sumac.
Alsike clover.
Goldenrod.
Aster.

Delaware:
Tulip poplar.
Crimson clover.
Tupelo.

Gallberry.
Persimmon.

Florida:
Tupelo.
Mangrove.
Thistle.
Orange.
Palmetto.
Sunflower.
Titi.

Georgia:
Tulip poplar.
Gallberry.
White and black
   tupelo.
Mexican-clover.
Sourwood.
Sumac.
Titi.

Idaho:
Alfalfa.
Sweetclover.
White clover.
Alsike clover.

Illinois:
Sweetclover.
White clover.
Heartsease.
Alsike clover.
Spanish needles.
Aster.
Basswood.

Indiana:
Alsike clover.
White clover.
Sweetclover.
Aster.
Tulip poplar.
Basswood.
Goldenrod.

Iowa:
Sweetclover.
White clover.
Alfalfa.
Alsike clover.
Basswood.

Heartsease.
Goldenrod.

Kansas:
White sweetclover.
Alfalfa.
White clover.
Heartsease.

Louisiana:
White clover.
Willow.
Peppervine.
Goldenrod.
Palmetto.
Vervain.

Maine:
Alsike clover.
Wild raspberry.
White clover.
Goldenrod.
Milkweed.

Maryland:
Alsike clover.
Tulip poplar.
White clover.
Locust.
Goldenrod.

Massachusetts:
Alsike clover.
Goldenrod.
White clover.
Blackberry and
   raspberry.
Fruit bloom.

Michigan:
Sweetclover.
White clover.
Alsike clover.
Basswood.
Buckwheat.
Goldenrod.
Alfalfa.

Minnesota:
Sweetclover.
White clover.
Alsike clover.
Basswood.

Montana:
Sweetclover.
Alfalfa.
Alsike clover.

Nebraska:
Sweetclover.
Alfalfa.
White clover.
Heartsease.
Goldenrod.

Nevada:
Alfalfa.
Sweetclover.
Sunflower.
Rabbitbrush.

New Jersey:
White clover.
Aster.
Sweetclover.
Alsike clover.
Goldenrod.
Sumac.

New York:
Alsike clover.
White clover.
Sweetclover.
Aster.
Goldenrod.
Buckwheat.
Sumac.
Alfalfa.
Basswood.

North Carolina:
Sourwood.
Tulip poplar.
Basswood.
Locust.
Sweetclover.
Black gum.
Tupelo.

North Dakota:
Sweetclover.

Ohio:
Alsike clover.
White clover.
Sweetclover.

Goldenrod.
Heartsease.
Alfalfa.
Missouri:
  White clover.
  Heartsease.
  Sweetclover.
  Spanish-needles.
  Alsike clover.
  Goldenrod.
  Basswood.
  Alfalfa.
  Aster.
  Goldenrod.
  Buckwheat.
Oklahoma:
  Sweetclover.
  Alfalfa.
  Horsemint.
  Cotton.
  Goldenrod.
  Heartsease.
Oregon:
  Alfalfa.
  Sweetclover.
  Fireweed.
  Alsike and white
    clover.
  Vetch.
Pennsylvania:
  Alsike clover.
  White clover.
  Aster.
  Locust.
  Buckwheat.
  Sweetclover.
  Goldenrod.
  Basswood.

South Carolina:
  Sourwood.
  Tuliptree.
  Basswood.
  Locust.
  Goldenrod.
  Sumac.
  Persimmon.
  Aster.
South Dakota:
  Sweetclover.
  Alfalfa.
  White clover.
Tennessee:
  White clover.
  Sourwood.
  Tulip poplar.
  Locust.
  Persimmon.
  Sweetclover.
  Thoroughwort.
  Goldenrod.
Texas:
  Cotton.
  Horsemint.
  Mesquite.
  Huajillo.
  Catclaw.
  Marigold.
Utah:
  Alfalfa.
  Sweetclover.
  Alsike clover.
  White clover.
Vermont:
  White clover.
  Basswood.
  Alsike clover.

Raspberry.
Goldenrod.
Alfalfa.
Virginia:
  White clover.
  Tulip poplar.
  Sourwood.
  Persimmon.
  Blueweed.
  Aster.
Washington:
  Fireweed.
  White clover.
  Alsike clover.
  Sweetclover.
  Alfalfa.
West Virginia:
  White clover.
  Sumac.
  Blue thistle.
  Tulip poplar.
  Basswood.
  Sourwood.
  Locust.
Wisconsin:
  White clover.
  Sweetclover.
  Alsike clover.
  Basswood.
  Alfalfa.
  Aster.
  Goldenrod.
Wyoming:
  Sweetclover.
  Alfalfa.
  Dandelion.
  Alsike clover.

Honey Research and Promotion Program, U.S. Department of Agriculture, Washington D.C., June, 1969.

native soil. Strong-tasting dark honeys, harvested in the summer and fall, are generally richest in iron and other minerals (see Table 2). Moreover, unprocessed, unfiltered honey contains tiny bits of pollen that are pure protein.[2] The inclusion of honey in the daily diet may help to eliminate a deficiency of trace elements.

Table 2. Amount of minerals in milligrams found in 250 grams of honey (approximately 1/2 pound) compared with Minimum Daily Requirement.

Constituents	Stringy Bark Dark (mg/250g)	Clover Light (mg/250g)	Adult M.D.R. (mg)
Silicon	5.75	34.00	
Aluminum	27.75	2.25	
Iron	9.25	2.25	12.00
Calcium	56.75	26.75	0.80
Magnesium	33.00	10.00	0.30
Sodium	2.75	62.75	10.00–20.00
Potassium	310.25	110.25	
Manganese	2.50	0.20	1.50
Copper	0.15	0.20	2.00
Chromium	0.15	0.075	
Nickel	0.015	0.075	
Zinc	0.05	0.75	12.00
Cobalt	1.50	0.05	15.00
Antimony	0.50	0.25	
Lead	0.05	0.025	
Phosphorus	30.75	32.25	1.30

(Established by V. Petrov, Royal Melbourne Institute of Technology, Melbourne)

Honey Processing

Honey is at its best in its unprocessed, natural state in which it is neither heated, filtered, nor clarified. However, these procedures often are employed in the commercial processing of honey.

2. Pollen, the reproductive male element of plants, is often sold separately from the honey; eaten alone, it has a slightly bitter taste. When blended with honey, it supplies one of nature's most concentrated sources of a whole range of micro-nutrients.

Heated Honey: Some commercial honey is inferior to freshly harvested honey because heat was improperly used to liquefy crystallized honey from the comb. Heating destroys enzymes and vitamins in honey. The only way to liquefy crystallized honey or to prevent crystallization is to heat it, but if precautions are not taken, heat can damage the flavor of honey. Even at a very low temperature, if the heat is raised too fast or maintained too long, the honey will darken and lose its delicate flavor. Knowledge of the thermal conductivity of honey is of practical importance. If granulated honey is liquefied by heat in large containers, the transmission of heat through the mass of honey is so slow that part of the honey can be overheated before the honey in the center is warmed enough to be liquefied.

Filtered Honey: The process of filtering takes out the pollen which contains protein. However, filtered honey, if it is not heated, retains its vitamins, minerals, and enzymes.

Clarified Honey: The combination of overheating and filtering honey will result in a clarified honey in which the enzymes and vitamins have been destroyed and the protein removed. Clarified honey often will remain in a liquid state and will not crystallize even at low temperatures.

Labeling

At present there is no standardized labeling for honey so the procedures used in commercial processing are not indicated on the label. However, the purity of honey is protected by federal laws. It is illegal to produce and label any product as honey that is not *pure* honey: imitations and honey blends cannot be sold as honey.

Grades and standards have been established by the United States Department of Agriculture and the Food and Drug Administration. The U.S.D.A. grades for honey are based on "flavor, color or clarity, moisture content, and freedom from defects." The F.D.A. standard for United States marketed honey is stated the following way:

"Honey is the nectar and saccharine exudation of plants, gathered, modified and stored in the comb of honey (*Apis mellifera* and *Apis dorsata*); it is levorotary and contains not more than 25% water, not more than 8% sucrose."

The standard moisture content of most honeys is 20%; the best honey, however, contains a maximum of 18% water.

The label *pure honey* or *honey* means that no foreign elements—beyond a permissible level of 8% pure sucrose—have been added to the honey. Thus, to obtain unprocessed honey, it is necessary to look for a

Smoker

Simple Extractor

Straight Knife

Tapered Knife

Spatula

Curved Knife

Wax Knife

Hive with handle for retreiving a Swarm

label that says not only "pure" or "natural," but also "raw," "uncooked," "unfiltered," or "organic."

Crystallized Honey

Because most honey is in a liquid state when purchased, many people think that crystallized or granulated honey is spoiled honey. This belief is totally erroneous. Crystallization allows the determination of purity and quality in honey. Pure, unprocessed honey will crystallize naturally over a period of time if it is left to stand in a container. With certain honeys, crystallization will occur very rapidly while still in the comb if the honey contains a relatively high level of glucose; it is the glucose that separates from water and crystallizes. Honey extracted from alfalfa will crystallize sooner than other types because of its substantial percentage of glucose; honey rich in fructose (levulose) will remain liquid longer. The difference in composition depends on the flowers visited by the bees.

Sometimes a white layer will form on top of crystallized honey as tiny air bubbles are squeezed to the surface. This does not mean that the honey is spoiled; pure, natural, raw honey will never spoil. Honey will not crystallize if the container is kept in a warm place but it will crystallize at low temperatures. To return honey to a liquid state, simply place the container in warm (not hot) water.

Spatula

Curved Knife

Wax Knife

Hive with handle for retreiving a Swarm

For so work the honey bees,
Creatures that by a rule in nature teach
The act of order to a peopled kingdom.
They have a king, and officers of sorts,
Where some like magistrates correct at home;
Others like merchants venture trade abroad;
Others like soldiers, armed in their stings,
Make boot upon the summer's velvet buds,
Which pillage they with merry march bring home
To the tent-royal of their emperor;
Who, busied in his majesty, surveys
The singing masons building roofs of gold,
The civil citizens kneading up the honey,
The poor mechanic porters crowding in
Their heavy burdens at his narrow gate,
The sad-ey'd justice, with his surly hum,
Delivering o'er to executors pale
The lazy, yawning drone.
—Shakespeare, *Henry V*

How Is Honey Made?

Nature's Contribution: *The Flower and the Bee*

The preparation of honey starts in the plant itself. The nectaries, two glands located near the base of the flower, secrete the nectar. Bees draw the nectar up through their long mouths and store it in their honey sacs where the processing of nectar starts immediately. The conversion of the nectar into honey is accomplished in two stages: first, by fermentation (produced by enzymes contained in the nectar itself and by enzymes extracted from the pharyngeal glands of the bees), and then, by evaporation of any excess moisture.

If the nectar is rich and abundant, it may take 900 bees one day to make a pound of honey; if the nectar's sugar content is low, however, it may take as long as 30 days for 3,000 bees to produce the same amount.

Apis mellifera, the common honey bee that was imported into the United States in the seventeenth century, is found throughout Europe, Australia, and Africa; *Apis dorsata*, the giant honeybee, is native to Asia. Because of FDA regulations, the honey of the other Asian species, *Apis*

15

cerana and *Apis horea*, cannot be sold in the United States. The honeybee is a social insect; it is also the tiniest domesticated creature. However, humans have never succeeded in modifying the basic behavior or physiology of the bee, and therefore, it operates in accordance with its inherent functions.

A colony of bees is composed of 75,000 to 90,000 bees living together and performing highly organized tasks. A colony may elect any cavity as a shelter either provided by nature (a hollow tree), or constructed by humans (a hive). As soon as they have moved into new quarters, the bees start building honeycombs with a wax that they exude from a series of plates located between the segments of their abdomens. Each comb is made of a double layer of hexagonal cells. The cells are constructed in two sizes: the smaller cells are used to store pollen or to rear worker bees, and the larger cells are used for honey storage and for rearing queen bees and male bees. A well-defined order prevails in the combs. The brood is lodged in the front of the central comb of the hive; in the outer parts are the cells filled with honey, and in between are the cells filled with pollen. The worker bees waterproof the nest with *propolis*, a resinous secretion collected from the surface of plants.

During the winter, the survival of the colony depends on the temperature maintained by the workers. When the temperature of the hive drops to 57° F., the workers form a compact cluster in the center of the hive. Some of the bees fill the vacant cells, while others place themselves in circles between the combs. The inner circles of bees produce heat by moving their legs, abdomens, and antennae; the outer circles form an insulating zone. If the temperature continues to drop, the bees fan their wings; should the temperature of the inner circle rise above 94°, then the cluster of bees loosens to allow warm air to escape. When the winter is over, brood rearing begins.

It was established in the early seventeenth century that the leader of the hive is a female—the queen bee—and not a king bee as Aristotle held. Queens and worker bees are genetically identical; their differentiation derives from their early nutrition. All female larvae are fed on "royal jelly" (a thick, milky secretion from the pharyngeal glands of "nursing" bees)[3] for the first three days, after which time the larvae that will become worker bees are fed "beebread" (a mixture of honey and

3. The unusual nature of royal jelly has prompted research into its chemical nature; the studies are not yet conclusive, but its high nutritional value has been recognized for centuries. Royal jelly contains protein:12.34%; lipides:5.46%; moisture:66.05%; reducing substances:12.49%; ash:0.82%; and undetermined components:2.84%; it is also a good source of vitamin B_1. Royal jelly is available in most health food stores.

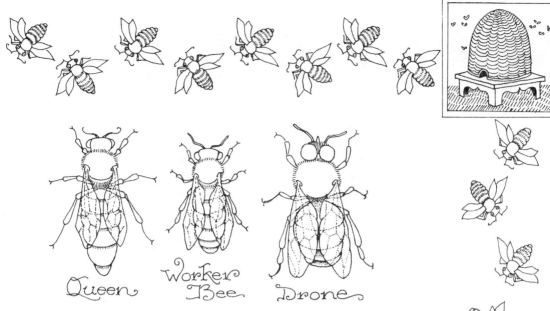

Queen   Worker Bee   Drone

pollen) until they hatch on the twenty-first day. In contrast, the queen larvae are fed only royal jelly and hatch within sixteen days. As soon as a mature queen emerges from her cell, she immediately destroys all the other queen larvae. If several queens mature at the same moment, a fight to the death occurs. The victor will be queen of the hive with a lifespan of four to five years.

After birth, the queen is allowed to wander about the hive, and for five to eight days, she draws little attention. Then the queen makes her initial mating flight from the hive and is followed by every drone (male bee) in the vicinity. The strongest and fastest drone mates with her high in the air and then dies. A queen will make an average of seven mating flights in her lifetime. After each flight, she retains the spermatozoa (in a special sac called the spermatheca) with which she fertilizes some of her eggs in order to produce female larvae (worker bees). A queen that has never mated can still lay unfertilized eggs that develop into the male drones.

During her lifetime each queen can produce more than a million eggs. In the spring, when the colony is building up, the queen will lay an egg per minute, day and night—a total of 1500 eggs that amounts to the weight of the queen herself. To lay eggs, the queen first examines a cell to make sure it is suitable; then she places her abdomen into it and lays an oblong egg which stands upright from the bottom of the cell. She is continuously pampered by attending worker bees, who caress her, feed her, clean her, and, if necessary, put her on a diet so that she will cease laying eggs and be light enough to wing away with the swarm.

Any erratic behavior on the queen's part however, such as laying two eggs in one cell, or being too weak to lay enough eggs, may cause the workers to become angry with their queen. They then will surround her, pull off her wings and her legs, and sting her to death. When a queen dies, the workers feed royal jelly to newly-layed larvae; but if the larvae

are more than three days old and have already been fed beebread, none can develop into a queen bee. The workers then will try to produce a queen by feeding royal jelly to other worker bees who will begin to lay eggs, but these unfertilized eggs will produce only male bees, the drones.

Drones develop in twenty-four days. Most of them die during the mating flight, while others die from starvation. Worker bees feed the drones as long as nectar is plentiful, but when the food supply drops in the fall, the workers drive the drones from the hive; homeless, none survive the winter.

Worker bees are female bees with undeveloped reproductive organs. They feed the brood, construct combs, clean the hive, guard against intruders, and collect the nectar and the pollen to make honey and wax. In which of these activities a worker bee will engage is usually determined by her age. When the young worker emerges from her cell, her job for the first week of life is to clean the brood cells, which will then be ready to receive new eggs. The following week she will act as a nursing bee and feed the larvae. Then she will pack pollen into cells by butting it with her head, or make wax and build combs. Only then will she become involved in the process of honey-making; however, she still will not be allowed to fly outside. Instead, she receives nectar from field bees, processes it in her honey sac, and stores it. (The worker bee has two stomachs; one to carry and process honey, the other for her own digestion.)

A worker bee can tell instinctively whether the nectar has the right degree of moisture. If it is too thin, she suspends it in droplets from the top of the cell and lets it dry; if it is too thick, she works it in her mouth until it reaches the proper texture (a concentration of about 60 percent sugar). Then she places it in the cells and starts the ripening process by fanning her wings until the excess moisture evaporates, leaving a sugar concentration of about 80 percent. This done, she seals the cell with wax so the honey will keep indefinitely.

After three weeks of hive work, the worker bee flies out to collect nectars and pollens discovered by the scout bee. The scout bees are an elite corps, but how they are selected is not known. Having found a food source (they are attracted by the ultraviolet fluorescence of nectar and pollen), they mark the source of food with an abdominally secreted hormone and return to the hive, noting the angle of their flight in relation to the sun. They then communicate the position of the flowers by performing a number of dances. According to Professor Karl Von Frisch (*The Dancing Bees*), the "wagging" dance indicates food at a distance, and the "round dance" indicates food near by. The scout bees also indicate the

Honey Stomach

kind of flowers by the scent of their body and by the nectar that they carry in their honey sacs. The drive of scout bees to find new sources of food depends entirely on the needs of the hive of which they apparently are well aware.

Field bees collect either nectar or pollen. (Collecting pollen is quicker than gathering nectar, so fewer bees are involved in this work.) When the food is abundant, worker bees can quickly die of exhaustion. Some of them fly with wings so worn that only stubs remain that barely carry their heavy load. Beekeepers have observed that when a bee falls exhausted, often other workers will revive her by placing a drop of nectar in her mouth, and she will wing away and resume her work. The life-span of a field bee depends on the type of labor she performs, but it seldom exceeds a few months.

When a colony becomes overpopulated and the brood area is over-crowded, the colony will divide by swarming. Queen cells are built and eggs are laid in them so that a new queen will emerge in time to head the population remaining in the hive. When the queen cells are ready and sealed, the old queen and most of the worker bees stream from the hive and fly in great circles until they find a support (such as a tree) on which the swarm can cluster while scout bees search for a cavity or hollow suitable as a new home. It is at this time that beekeepers are able to capture a swarm and carry it to a prepared hive. Today, most beekeepers' hives are built so that extra space is available when the bees require it, thus avoiding the swarming that will divide a colony.

He who loves honey should be patient with the stinging of the bees.

—Moorish proverb

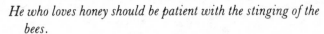

The Human Factor: *Beekeeping*

Bees are an essential part of the ecological cycle; honey production can be a great boon to organic farming because bees help to pollenate so many crops by carrying the pollen that is the fertilizing element in seed or fruit plants. For anyone who is well informed, beekeeping can be very easy and very enjoyable. One hive takes about one hour of care per week. The harvest will depend on several factors: the bees themselves, the availability of nectar, the climate, and the weather.

Beekeeping requires space (bees forage in a radius of 1-2 miles) and abundant nectar-producing plants. Hives should be set up in an isolated place where the bees will not be a nuisance to people or to animals. The beginner's equipment should include the hives, complete with chambers in which honey is collected; a smoker (which is used to make the bees harmless when it is necessary to work the inside of the hive); a veil or a net, to protect the face; special gloves; and a long spatula with which to collect the combs.

Late spring is the time to buy bees, which generally come in a specially ventilated box containing larvae, about 200 drones, 1,500 worker bees, a queen bee, and combs filled with honey, the food for the colony. An experienced beekeeper's help is needed to set up the hive and transfer the packaged bees.

Local beekeeping associations can provide referrals and information to the novice beekeeper. In addition, the American Beekeeping Federation holds annual conventions, and the International Federation of Apicultural Associations has headquarters in Rome (at Corso Vittorio Emanuele 101). Several specialized publications offer information on various aspects of beekeeping. The *American Bee Journal* (published monthly in Hamilton, Illinois 62341) is an excellent source; *ABJ* can be found in libraries and is also available on microfilm from University Microfilm, Inc. (Ann Arbor, Michigan 48103). Many people, having taken up beekeeping as a hobby, find it a profitable business with many ecological benefits.

The origin of bees is from Paradise
and it is because of man's sin they came
and God gave his blessing to them.
— Welsh proverb

Honey in Myth and History

Bees were making honey long before mankind appeared on Earth. Petrified bees have been found in geological strata antedating the oldest human skeletal remains, and fossilized bees have been found in amber. Moreover, prehistoric peoples used honey as food. Their rock paintings clearly depict the harvest of wild honey by men armed with long sticks. The earliest rock painting of this sort, dating from as early as 7000 B.C., was discovered in eastern Spain. Honey-gathering must have been equally common in Africa: a rock painting discovered in Rhodesia shows a gatherer using smoke to protect himself against the bees while he robs their nest.

In the Bronze Age, the use of honey and beeswax began to spread considerably, and the plunder of wild bee-nests no longer sufficed. People's needs made them ingenious. There is ample evidence that beeswax was used to cast metal artifacts, and that it was used on writing tablets; it also served as putty, and was mixed in medicinal preparations and in cosmetics. The honey bee became the only insect, out of 750,000 species, to be domesticated. When the hunter-gatherers became farmers, they produced the honey crop by attracting swarms of bees into prepared *skeps* — primitive beehives made of mud only, mud and straw, or hollow tree trunks. The bees accepted the living space provided by these primitive farmers and have remained dependable throughout thousands of years of beekeeping.

Bees are depicted in Egyptian hieroglyphics that date back some 6,000 years, and various reliefs show the harvesting of honey from clay hives that are very similar to the hives still being used along the Nile today. The Ancient Egyptians' technique was quite advanced. They developed a migratory beekeeping by which boats were loaded with hives in Upper Egypt and, as they floated slowly down the Nile, the bees foraged along the river bank, following the blossoming of the flowers. By the time the hives reached Memphis, the honey was ready to be

21

Spatula

Curved Knife

Wax Knife

Hive with handle for retreiving a Swarm

Smoker

Simple Extractor

Straight Knife

Tapered Knife

harvested. This practice is still followed today in Florida: bees are transported up and down the Apalachicola River so they can forage among the tupelo trees in bloom.

Sealed jars of honey have been found in several pharaohs' tombs: honey dating back to 3,000 B.C. has been tested and found to be pure and edible. The Egyptians knew that nothing would spoil in pure honey—a fact since confirmed by modern science—thus it is easy to understand why they used honey to embalm their dead. The Egyptians also considered honey an eternal food to be left forever in the sealed tombs so that the dead might be nourished in the afterlife; because honey does not spoil, it was associated with immortality and resurrection. As the only incorruptible food known, honey also was considered fit for the gods, and served as an offering in Egyptian religious ceremonies.

Because the Egyptians sacralized honey, the Hebrews were forbidden to offer up honey to Yaweh; however, the Jewish High Priest would accept honey as a tithe. And today, according to tradition, when an Orthodox Jewish boy of five begins to learn how to read, a drop of honey is placed on the first page of the book in a custom associating learning and sweetness that originated in Biblical times.

References to honey as the best and sweetest food abound in the Bible: indeed, the Promised Land is described as flowing with milk and honey. The honeybee may, in fact, have originated in India since the word for honey in Sanskrit is *madhu;* in Greek, it is *methu;* and in Anglo-Saxon, *medu,* which ultimately gives us *mead.* The Rig-Veda (the sacred book of India, compiled between 3,000 and 2,000 B.C.) often refers to

22   The Book of Honey

bees: the three gods, Vishnu, Krishna, and Indra, are called "the nectar-born." Vishnu's attributes are symbolized by the lotus surmounted by a bee.

Ancient lore indicates how highly humanity has regarded this unique insect which makes the sweetest and most sustaining of all foods. In Greek mythology, the infant Zeus—destined to be the most powerful of the gods—was fed honey by the bees. In Finnish mythology, the bee was chosen from all creation to be the messenger that will fly to the moon to bring honey and the prayers of the people to the Creator. The Germanic tribes believed that thunderstorms happened when the god of thunder came to steal honey.

One of the books of the Koran is devoted to the bee; the insect is taught by the Lord how to make honey. The prophet Mohammed says that the bee is the only creature ever directly addressed by the Lord. He says, moreover, that "Honey is a remedy for all illnesses." In the fifth century B.C., Hippocrates, the Greek physician, prescribed honey for longevity, and many Greeks who believed in perfecting the body and soul made honey an important part of their daily diet. Greek athletes ate honey as a quick energy food and drank honey mixed with water to relieve fatigue. The Pythagoreans' diet contained a generous amount of honey; they considered it the perfect natural food.

The Romans also believed that honey belonged in the daily diet of

Honey in Myth and History 23

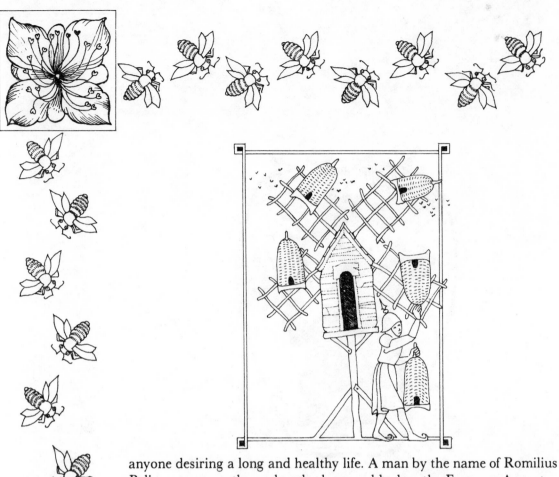

anyone desiring a long and healthy life. A man by the name of Romilius Polion was more than a hundred years old when the Emperor Augustus (63 B.C.-14 A.D.) came to dine with him. Amazed by his host's fitness, the emperor asked Romilius Polion how he managed to remain in such good shape. "Eat honey and rub your body with oil," was the wise man's answer. Pliny the Elder (23-79 A.D.) reported in his *Natural History* that he found very old people among beekeepers. Indeed, he had found 124 individuals who ate honey every day and had passed their hundredth birthday.

In his cookbook, *De Re Coquinaria*, Apicius, a famous Roman gourmet of the first century A.D., gives a very good idea of how honey was used in Roman cuisine. During a typical banquet (an affair that usually lasted several hours and sometimes through the night), first came the *gustus* (the equivalent of today's appetizers or hors-d'oeuvres) served with honeywine. These delicacies included: jellyfish and eggs; sow's udders stuffed with salted sea urchins; patina of brains cooked with milk, eggs, and honey; boiled tree fungi with peppered fish fat sauce; spiced sea urchins with honey, oil, and egg sauce. The *cena*, or dinner, might feature the following courses: fallow deer roasted with onion sauce, rue, Jericho dates, raisins, oil, and honey; boiled ostrich with honey sweet sauce; turtle dove boiled in its feathers; roast parrot; dormice stuffed with pork, pine kernels, and honey; ham boiled with figs and bay leaves, rubbed with honey, and baked in a pastry crust;

24　The Book of Honey

flamingo boiled with dates and honey. Desserts included: fricassée of roses with honey and pastry; stoned dates stuffed with nuts and pine kernels, fried in honey; and hot African sweet-wine cake with honey.

Indeed, honey was so popular in the Roman Empire that it was served with wine everywhere. In the ruins of Pompeii, traces of honey were found in the bottom of all the cups in the taverns. Honey was consumed in such quantities throughout the empire that it became scarce, the price was inflated, and it became a delicacy for the wealthy. (The poor were forced to make do with a substitute: date honey made of crushed dates slightly fermented in water.) At a banquet held for Nero, the cost of honey reached 400,000 sesterces—an astronomical price. Honey became so valuable that it was often demanded in tribute from defeated enemies. The small island of Corsica, for example, was required to deliver 200,000 pounds of honey to the Romans each year.

No wonder the Romans were so eager to invade Britain, which they called "an island of honey." Beekeeping was already prevalent throughout the British Isles, an industry that continued to grow through the centuries. Skeps could be found everywhere, on farms and in small gardens within the walls of fortified towns.

During the war-torn Middle Ages, before the invention of guns and cannons, the abundant hives were suddenly pressed into service—as weapons. When the Danes besieged the city of Chester in the tenth century, the townspeople responded by hurling rocks, pitch, and boiling oil

from the fortifications. However, the Danes set up sturdy hurdles covered with thick skins and proceeded to tunnel beneath the town walls. The people of Chester began to lose heart until someone came up with a novel weapon: the bee-bomb. In the dead of the night, the townspeople placed their hives atop the walls and, on a signal, precipitated them onto the unsuspecting Danes. The angry bees poured out in swarms, forcing the Danes to flee in pain and panic. Bee-bombs were so effective as a weapon that before long the technique was improved by the invention of a skep-flinging windmill. This device, which can be seen in miniature paintings on ancient manuscripts, would project hives over town walls, dispersing everyone in sight.

Thus, bees have long been used as allies in warfare. The Crusaders used them against the Saracens; they even were used at sea against enemy ships. As late as the Civil War, the North employed bees like pigeons to carry messages attached to their bodies through the Confederate lines.

Although there has been much speculation concerning the introduction of bees and beekeeping in the United States, there is little evidence to support the contention that there was ever a native honey bee. On the contrary, all evidence points to its having come from Europe with the colonists. John Josselyn, a traveler who resided in New England in 1638, noted that the honeybees were carried over by the English and thrived in America.

And nature, itself, contributed to the bees' spread: in 1670, a hurricane carried swarms of bees from New England over the Allegheny Mountains opening the West to the winged colonists. Settlers apparently brought the honeybee to Pensacola, Florida, in 1763, and it is assumed that the Spaniards must have imported the honeybee to the east Coast of Florida even earlier.

In a paper published by the American Philosophical Society in 1973, Benjamin Barton pointed out that the Indians had no word for war or honey; in fact, they called the bee "the White man's fly." The Indians apparently did not condone the colonists' utilitarianism; a popular native saying went, "White man works, makes horse work, makes ox work, now makes fly work."

*. . . a country like your own, a land
of corn and good wine, a land of bread and of vineyards, a
land of oil and of honey, so that you may not die but live.*
—2 Kings

Honey as Medicine and Cosmetic

Honey is, first and foremost, a high-energy food, good for people engaged in strenuous physical or intellectual work. Taken in small amounts, honey acts as a source of direct nutrition for the blood, the heart, the muscles, and the brain.

The average person burns up 1 ounce of sugar per hour. Since the nervous system is dependent upon a constant sugar supply for optimal functioning, the blood sugar must always be maintained at a level over one tenth of one percent of the blood to keep the brain and the central nervous system functioning. Sugar is transformed by the body into glucose. Honey is a super-saturated solution of predigested sugars that is easily absorbed and used by the body for energy. First, the glucose portion of honey is quickly absorbed into the blood stream. Then the levulose or fructose is changed first to glycogen and then to dextrose (glucose), in a process that gives honey an extended as well as an immediate energizing effect.

Honey's power to provide quick energy has been recognized for millennia. The Bible (1 Sam. 14:27) recounts that Jonathan "stretched out the stick that was in his hand, dipped the end of it in the honeycomb, put it to his mouth and was refreshed."

Through the ages, honey also has been prized for its mild antibiotic properties and used in myriad pharmaceutical preparations designed to treat everything from rickets, scurvy, anemia, inflammation of the intestine, dropsy, constipation, rheumatism, migraine headaches, and dizziness, to disfunctions of the liver and the stomach. It has also been prescribed for infants as well as for people with weak digestive systems or those who lack the two enzymes invertose and amylase necesary for the process of sugar inversion. Furthermore, honey is the sugar best handled by the kidneys.

Honeycomb has been chewed through the centuries to relieve disorders of the breathing tract; it sooths and desensitizes the bronchia and also appears to be an anti-allergen. One explanation is the presence of

pollen. Folk medicine recommends that people suffering from allergy to pollens (such as hay-fever) chew local honeycomb on a regular basis as soon as it becomes available in the spring.

Honey packs, placed on wounds and burns, have been a traditional dressing since antiquity, providing prompt relief from pain and itching. Honey's germ-killing effects are attributed to its capacity to absorb water; bacteria trapped in it perish from lack of moisture. Honey's bactericidal power is further increased by the fact that honey is acid in reaction and contains potassium, making it an unfavorable medium for the growth of bacteria. Dr. D. C. Jarvis in *Folk Medicine* (Fawcett, 1958), cites experiments in which various germs, placed in pure honey, soon died.

Certain medicinal properties are attributed to various types of honey. Since almost every honey is a blend of many floral nectars, the honey must contain at least 51 percent of the nectar of a particular flower in order to be labeled as a honey of a specific floral origin.

Alfalfa, Clover, Sainfoin, and Colza Honey: Made from nectar gathered in fields, the honey has a pale, golden color, a delicate flavor, and soothing, relaxing properties. The proportion of the different nectars in this honey will vary from year to year, and with it the consistency and color. When sainfoin prevails, the honey is a granulous, rich gold. When alfalfa prevails, the honey is white and smooth. When colza prevails, the honey crystallizes very rapidly.

Buckwheat Honey: A dark, very viscous honey that sets to a jell-like consistency, it becomes liquid again when stirred, and resets when allowed to stand. Containing many trace minerals, the honey is highly nutritious and helps to restore health and strength.

Clover Honey: Smooth, light amber in color, with a sweet, light taste, this honey acts as a soothing tonic. It is recommended for young children.

Chestnut Honey: Deep amber, with a strong flavor, the honey stimulates blood circulation and also is helpful in curing dysentery.

Eucalyptus Honey: With its strong, specific flavor, this honey is used in the treatment of respiratory infections; it also disinfects the urinary tract.

Heather Honey: The honey has a rusty color and crystallizes very rapidly. Kept in a jar, it turns into round crystals 1–2 mm. in diameter. It becomes liquid again when stirred, and resets when left to stand. Containing easily assimilable iron, this honey is an energy booster. It also has a tonic effect on the heart, and contains diuretic properties.

Honey-Locust Honey: Liquid in consistency, golden in color, and light in fragrance, the honey has a relaxing effect on the nervous system and is considered an especially good energy booster.

Lavender Honey: Clear and translucent, with a specific and very pleasant flavor, this honey has anti-spasmodic and tonic properties that alleviate stubborn coughs and laryngitis.

Linden Honey: Light in color and delicate in flavor, the honey is used as a sedative, an anti-spasmodic, and a relaxant. It is said to relieve headaches and also to soothe the digestive tract.

Mountain Honey: Nectars gathered at high altitudes produce a honey prized as an antidote to the common cold.

Orange Blossom Honey: This pale amber honey is very sweet and has a pleasant aroma. It is useful in cases of insomnia caused by digestive problems.

Pinetree Honey: A dark honey which remains liquid for a very long time after harvesting, the honey has a resinous flavor and is considered good for the treatment of bronchial inflammation.

Rosemary Honey: Light amber and flavorful, the honey is prescribed for liver conditions; it is reputed to be a stimulant.

Sage Honey: This pale amber, delicately flavored honey remains fluid long after the harvest. Like sage tea, it is used as a tonic and stimulant.

Honey has also been used as a cosmetic since antiquity. To this day it is still used in hand and body lotions, facial creams, soaps and depilatories. Honey penetrates tiny crevices through which water will not pass and thus makes an excellent emollient as well as a protective germ-proof shield.

Smoker

Simple Extractor

Straight Knife

Tapered Knife

Spatula

Curved Knife

Wax Knife

Hive with handle for retreiving a Swarm

Being anointed with honey live sweetly.
— Erasmus: Colloquia

Medicinal Preparations

Nervous Conditions

Insomnia

Honey can be used as a sedative. If falling asleep at night is difficult, take 1 tablespoon of honey at your evening meal. Should sleeping problems continue, try one of the following two mixtures.

(1) 2 teaspoons apple vinegar
2 teaspoons honey
1 glass water

Combine the ingredients and take 1/4 cup at bedtime.

(2) 3 teaspoons cider vinegar
1 cup honey
1 quart water

Combine the ingredients in a bottle and mix well. Take two teaspoons at bedtime. Repeat after 1 hour, if necessary.

Lethargy

2 egg yolks
1/4 cup honey
1 ounce sherry

Combine the ingredients in a blender. Chill before using.

Circulatory, Digestive, and Respiratory Ailments

Hangover

1/2 cup honey
1/2 cup grapefruit
Crushed ice

Combine the ingredients and take at bedtime to prevent a hangover.
Note: One tablespoon of honey before a party can neutralize some of the effects of alcohol.

Muscle Cramps

Take two teaspoons of honey at each meal for a week. If there is a tendency for muscle cramp to recur, at least 2 tablespoons of honey should be made a part of the daily diet.

For muscular pain, spread honey over the painful area, cover with gauze, then place a piece of flannel over the gauze. Allow the area to remain covered for 2 hours. If necessary, repeat the application and allow to remain covered for another 2 hours.

Spatula

Constipation

2 tablespoons honey, every day.

A natural, mild laxative, honey will not produce gastric disturbances. If part of the daily diet, it will prevent constipation.

Ozimeli (for fever)

1/3 cup honey
1/3 cup sea water
1/3 cup vinegar
1 teaspoon sea salt

Curved Knife

Wax Knife

Combine the ingredients. Take as needed to reduce fever.

Thalassomeli (for poisons)

1/3 cup honey
1/3 cup rain water
1/3 cup sea water

Combine the ingredients. Take as needed to induce vomiting.

Hive with handle for retreiving a Swarm

Allergies and Congestion

Chewing local honeycomb is an effective anti-congestant for stuffy nose or nasal sinusitis; it is also effective in eliminating allergies such as hayfever. Chew 1 piece of local honeycomb for 15 minutes; discard the remains. Repeat 4 to 6 times a day as necessary for up to 15 days.

Asthma

1 small onion
2 garlic cloves
1 pint of Irish Moss Jelly
1/2 cup honey

Simmer the onion and garlic in the Irish Moss Jelly for 30 minutes.

Allow the mixture to cool, then strain; add the honey to the strained jelly.

Alternate taking 1 tablespoon of the jelly-honey mixture and 1 tablespoon of honey at 2 hour intervals.

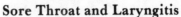

Sore Throat and Laryngitis

Hot milk with honey soothes the throat and helps to restore the voice. Try one of the following recipes.

(1) 1 tablespoon honey
     8 ounces milk

Heat the milk (do not boil) in a small pan. Pour into a cup or glass and add the honey.

(2) 1 egg white
     1/2 cup West Indian Honey Gulakund

Beat the egg white until stiff peaks form, then blend in the honey. Take as needed to soothe a sore throat. (Gulakund also can be taken to settle the stomach.)

Cough

      1 lemon
      1 cup honey
      2 tablespoons glycerin

Boil the lemon in water to cover for 10 minutes or until the rind softens; then cut in half and extract juice. Pour the lemon juice into a glass; add the glycerine and honey, mixing well. Take one teaspoon every 4 hours. As the coughing spells become less frequent, increase the time between doses.

How doth the little busy bee
Improve each shining hour,
And gather honey all the day
From every opening flower.
— Isaac Watts: *Divine Songs for Children*

XVIII Century Recipes

Violet Honey

1 cup of fresh violets
3 cups of honey

Pour the honey over the violets and place in a hot area for 8 days. Then place the mixture in a large pan and bring to a medium boil; continue boiling until mixture reduces by 1/4. Press the mixture through a sieve, then return to the pan and cook until syrupy, skimming the foam carefully. Take 1 tablespoon as needed to relieve constipation and stomachache.

Water Lily Honey

1 cup of fresh water lilies
3 cups of honey

Pour the honey over the water lilies and place in a hot area for 8 days. Then place the mixture in a large pan and bring to a medium boil; continue boiling until mixture reduces by 1/4. Press the mixture through a sieve, then return to the pan and cook until syrupy, skimming the foam carefully.

Take 1 tablespoon as needed to relieve migraines and headaches.

Garden Mercury Honey

1/2 cup of juice of garden mercury
1/2 cup honey

Combine ingredients in a pan and simmer until syrupy. Take 1 tablespoon twice a day for constipation, dropsy, or rheumatism.

The Long-Life Honey Syrup

   2 pounds juice of garden mercury
   1/2 pound juice of borage
   1/2 pound juice of bugloss
   2 ounces gladioli roots or orris roots, crushed
   1 ounce root of gentian, crushed
   2 pounds of honey
   12 ounces white wine

Marinate the crushed roots in the wine overnight. Melt the honey over low heat; add the juices. Boil 1 minute, skim the foam; pour through a sieve. Combine the crushed roots and liquid mixture in a pan over low heat and simmer until a heavy syrup forms.

   Take 3 hours before meals to relieve migraines and dizziness. The syrup retains its potency for approximately 2 weeks.

Honey Rosemary

   1 cup fresh rosemary flowers
   3 cups honey

Combine the ingredients in a covered jar and place in the sun or in a hot place for one month. Then add a little water, to cover the ingredients, place over heat and simmer for 15 minutes. Strain through a sieve into a container.

   The syrup, which retains its potency for approximately 2 weeks, is good for the liver and the stomach.

See how much brighter my eyes are now that I have eaten this mouthful of honey.

—1 Samuel

Cosmetic Preparations

Basic Body-Care

Hair Conditioner

2 tablespoons honey
1 tablespoon olive oil

Combine the ingredients in a bowl. Apply to the hair and scalp and massage for at least 3 minutes. Warm the hair with a hair dryer set on low (or sit outdoors in the sun) to help the lotion penetrate. Allow the mixture to remain on the hair for 20 to 30 minutes, then wash with a good shampoo.

French Honey Soap

4 ounces castille soap flakes
4 ounces honey
1/2 ounce tartaric salt
1/4 ounce fumitory water

Combine the ingredients in a pan and place over low heat until the mixture thickens. Pour into small molds and allow to cool. Use as a toilet soap.

Face Mask (for oily or normal skin)

1 fresh egg white
1 tablespoon of dry milk
1 teaspoon of honey

Combine the ingredients in a bowl using a whisk, or place in a blender at low speed for 2 minutes or until creamy. Apply the cream to the face and throat allowing it to remain on the skin for 15 minutes. Remove the mask with warm water; follow with an application of cold water.

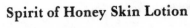

Spirit of Honey Skin Lotion

This skin lotion for the face and the body is a good conditioner for both normal and dry skin.

    1 cup honey
    1 teaspoon coriander
    1 teaspoon lemon rind
    1 clove
    A dash of nutmeg
    1/2 teaspoon benzoin
    1/2 teaspoon calamite lotion
    1 vanilla bean
    2 cups rose water
    2 cups orange flower water

Place the ingredients in a glass container. Cover tightly and allow to stand at room temperature in a dark place for 1 week. Shake the container several times during the week to mix the ingredients. Strain and pour into a quart-sized bottle. Use after bathing or in the bathwater.

Blemishes

Honey and almond butter can be used on the skin as an abrasive to eliminate blackheads and skin impurities.

    1/4 cup honey
    1/4 cup almond butter
    A sprinkling of finely chopped almonds

Combine the ingredients in a bowl, mixing well. Gently rub the mixture over the face and throat with the tips of the fingers. Rinse with lukewarm water.

Canker Sores

    1/4 cup honey
    1/4 cup lemon

Take a teaspoon of the mixture and hold it as long as you can in your mouth without swallowing. Repeat at least twice a day until the symptoms subside.

Dry Skin

Honey Lotion

> 1 tablespoon honey
> 2 tablespoons water

Combine the ingredients in a small cup. Apply to heal chapped hands. If used regularly, this mixture will condition the skin and prevent chapping.

Honey and Glycerine

> 1/4 cup honey
> 1/4 cup glycerine

Combine ingredients in a bowl, mixing well. Store in a bottle and use as an emollient for dry skin.

Honey Mask (for dry skin)

> 1 teaspoon of honey
> 1 teaspoon of rye flour
> 1 teaspoon of olive oil
> 1 egg yolk

Combine the ingredients in a small bowl and mix well. Cover the face and throat with the mixture, allowing it to remain on the skin for 30 minutes. Remove with lukewarm water.

Anti-Wrinkle Mask

> 1 teaspoon of honey
> 1 teaspoon of onion juice
> 1 teaspoon of beeswax
> 1 lily bulb, washed and crushed

Combine the ingredients in a double-boiler and warm until the beeswax is melted, mixing with a wooden spatula until smooth. Allow the mixture to cool, then apply to the face and throat for 30 minutes. Remove with lukewarm water.

Smoker

Simple Extractor

Straight Knife

Tapered Knife

Spatula

Curved Knife

Wax Knife

Hive with handle for retreiving a Swarm

*Honey is like the morning sun
It has all the grace of summer
And the mellow freshness of the fall*
—Garcia Lorca

Cooking with Honey

Natural honey is raw honey taken directly from the honey comb and unadulterated in any way. The recipes in this book refer to raw honey, only.

Basic Cooking Information

- Because of its high acid content, honey should never be stored or handled in copper or zinc containers; aluminum should also be avoided. Tin, stainless steel, or glass are recommended.
- Honey does not require refrigeration and will not spoil at room temperature.
- Honey should be stored in a dry place since it absorbs and retains moisture.
- When measuring honey, coat the cup or spoon with a little oil and the honey will not stick.
- Honey is sweeter than sugar. One teaspoon of honey has the sweetness of 1 1/2 teaspoons of sugar.
- High temperatures affect the flavor of honey, so baked products should be baked for a longer period of time at lower temperatures, 315°–350°F.
- Cakes, puddings, cookies, and candies will stay fresh and moist longer when made with honey.

Equivalents: Weights and Measures

1 teaspoon	=	20 calories		
1 tablespoon	=	3 teaspoons	=	60 calories
1 ounce	=	2 tablespoons		
1/4 cup	=	4 tablespoons		
1/3 cup	=	5 1/3 tablespoons		
1/2 cup	=	8 tablespoons		
1 cup	=	16 tablespoons = 8 fluid ounces = 1/2 pint		
1 pint	=	2 cups		
1 quart	=	2 pints = 4 cups		
1 gram	=	1/30 ounce		
1 kilo	=	2.20 pounds		
1 liter	=	1 quart (approximate)		

Spatula

Substitutions

Honey contains 18 to 20 percent water. If you want to substitute honey for sugar in your own recipes, use 1 1/2 fluid ounces (3 tablespoons) less of the liquid (water or milk) called for by the recipe. When substituting sugar with honey in baked goods, add 1/2 teaspoon baking soda for every cup of honey.

Curved Knife

Wax Knife

1 cup granulated white sugar (equals 1 cup brown sugar, firmly packed, or 1 1/3 cups granulated brown sugar) = 1 cup honey less 3 tablespoons liquid in recipe

1 cup fresh milk = 1/2 cup dry milk + 1/2 cup water

1 cup buttermilk or sourmilk = 1 tablespoon of lemon juice or vinegar in 1 cup of milk

2 tablespoons of flour = 1 tablespoon cornstarch

1 teaspoon baking powder = 1/4 teaspoon soda + 1/2 teaspoon cream of tartar.

Hive with handle for retreiving a Swarm

The House of Israel named it 'manna.' It was like coriander seed; it was white and its taste was like that of wafers made with honey.

> —Exodus

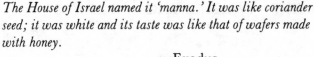

Basic Recipes

Milk Stock

MAKES 1 QUART

4 cups water
1 cup fresh milk
1 lemon, sliced in thin rounds
1 teaspoon dark honey
A dash of sea salt and pepper

Place all ingredients in a deep pan and bring to a gentle boil. Simmer over low heat for 10 minutes, stirring constantly with a wooden spoon.

Vegetable Stock

MAKES 2 QUARTS

10 cups water
3 medium onions, chopped
2 stalks of celery, chopped
3 carrots, sliced in rounds
1 teaspoon thyme
2 bay leaves
3 sprigs of parsley
2 cups red wine vinegar
1 tablespoon honey
A dash of sea salt

Place all ingredients in a deep pan and bring to a boil; reduce heat and simmer for 60 minutes. Remove pan from the heat and allow to cool for 5 minutes. Strain through a fine-mesh strainer, reserving the liquid.

Chicken Stock

MAKES 2 QUARTS

    2 pounds leftover chicken bones
    10 cups water
    1 medium onion, minced
    3 carrots, sliced into thin rounds
    1 cup fresh celery, chopped
    1/2 small head of lettuce, shredded
    5 eggshells

Chop chicken bones into 2-inch lengths and place in a deep pan with water and the next 4 ingredients. Bring to a boil, then reduce heat and simmer for 60 minutes, skimming any debris from the surface. Return to a rolling boil, and drop in the eggshells, again skimming any debris. When the stock is clear, remove from heat; cool and strain, reserving the liquid.

Fish Stock

MAKES 2 QUARTS

Use either white or red-fleshed fish trimmings, but never use them together in the same preparation. For a stronger stock, add pieces of fish meat in addition to the trimmings.

    4 cups fish trimmings: heads, tails, et cetera
    10 cups water
    1/2 cup white wine vinegar
    1 medium onion, minced
    3 carrots, sliced into thin rounds
    1 clove
    5 parsley sprigs
    1 teaspoon fennel seeds

Combine the ingredients in a large pan and bring to a boil; reduce heat and cook for 40 to 50 minutes, skimming off any debris that surfaces. Turn off the heat and allow the stock to cool. Strain, reserving the liquid.

Basic Recipes 41

Garlic Stock

MAKES 1 QUART

6 cups water
4 garlic cloves, minced
2 bay leaves
A dash of sea salt
1 tablespoon sage leaves
2 tablespoons olive oil

Combine the water, garlic, bay leaves, and salt, in a large pan and bring to a boil; reduce heat and simmer for 15 minutes. Remove pan from heat and add the sage; allow the stock to cool for 5 minutes. Strain through a fine-mesh strainer into a non-metallic bowl. Now stir in the olive oil.

Note: Do not boil the sage or the oil lest they become bitter.

Homemade Tomato Paste (Coulis)

MAKES 1 CUP

In Mediterranean countries, a pot of "coulis" is always ready in the refrigerator to use with rice or pasta, or to serve as a base for sauce.

8 medium tomatoes
12 peppercorns
2 garlic cloves, halved
1 teaspoon thyme
1 bay leaf, crushed
1 tablespoon honey
1 teaspoon sea salt

Drop the tomatoes into enough vigorously boiling water to cover, and boil for 1 minute. Then peel and quarter the tomatoes and place in a large pan with water to cover. Add the remaining ingredients and simmer, covered, for 2 to 3 hours, depending on the desired thickness. To store, place in an airtight jar and keep refrigerated.

Rice

White Rice: Place 1 cup of white rice and 2 cups of water into a saucepan; bring to a rolling boil and stir with a wooden spoon. Reduce heat, cover, and simmer for 15 minutes. Do not lift the lid or stir while the rice is cooking.

Brown Rice: Place 2 1/2–3 cups of water in pan and bring to a boil. Add 1 cup brown rice; reduce heat, cover, and simmer for 30 to 40 minutes or until the water is absorbed.

Pressure-cooked Rice: Combine 1 cup of rice with one cup of water in a pressure-cooker; bring to pressure, then reduce heat and simmer for 15 minutes. Remove from the heat; allow the pan to stand 4 to 5 minutes until the pressure returns to normal.

Wild Rice: Place 1 cup of well–washed wild rice in a pan with 2 1/2 cups of water. Bring to a gentle boil; reduce heat and simmer uncovered about 45 minutes or until all the water is absorbed.

The king was in his counting-house
Counting out his money;
The queen was in the parlour,
Eating bread and honey.
　　　　　　—Nursery Rhyme

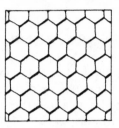

Breads and Muffins

Homemade breads have a matchless aroma. Honey adds flavor and moisture, and the bread retains its freshness for a longer period of time. Gluten, a nutritious protein substance found in wheat and other grains, causes dough to rise when combined with yeast. Wheat, oat, rye, buckwheat, and barley are gluten flours that can be substituted one for another in recipes to make yeast-leavened, high protein breads. Flours such as corn, rice, millet, soya bean, and peanut do not contain gluten and require baking powder and baking soda for the bread to rise.

The most flavorful breads are made when two kinds of flour are mixed together. When the dough becomes too stiff to stir with a spoon, use your hands to work the ingredients together.

Honey Rye-Wheat Bread

MAKES 2 ROUND LOAVES

2 cups warm milk
1 teaspoon sea salt
1/3 cup vegetable oil
1/3 cup honey
1 cake dry yeast, crumbled
3 1/2 cups whole wheat flour
2 cups rye flour

Combine the first 4 ingredients in a large bowl; add the crumbled yeast and mix well. Add the whole wheat and the rye flours a little at a time, mixing well after each addition. Turn the dough onto a lightly floured board, allowing it to stand for 5 minutes. Knead the dough for approximately 8 minutes until it attains an elastic texture. Coat a large mixing bowl with oil. Place the ball of dough in the bowl, turning it until evenly coated with oil; cover with a cloth and allow it to rise in a warm place (80°) for 2 hours or until its bulk has doubled.

Punch down the dough and reshape into a ball, allowing it to rise again for 45 minutes. Punch down once more and divide the dough into two balls, allowing them to stand for 15 minutes. Place the balls of dough on a greased baking sheet; cover with a cloth and allow to rise until double in size (1 to 1 1/2 hours).

Preheat oven to 375°. Bake for 45 minutes or until browned. Allow the bread to cool before slicing.

French Gingerbread

MAKES 1 LOAF

1/2 pound unbleached white flour
1/2 teaspoon baking soda
1/2 teaspoon anise seeds
1 cup milk
1/4 cup honey

Combine the first four ingredients in a bowl, blending until smooth. Allow the batter to stand overnight.

Preheat oven to 325°. Stir the honey into the batter, mixing well; pour the batter into a 9–inch loaf pan. Bake for 60 minutes or until a knife inserted into the center of the cake comes out clean. Allow to cool and serve plain or topped with a honey spread.

Breads and Muffins 45

Spatula

Curved Knife

Wax Knife

Hive with handle for retrieving a Swarm

Two Flours Bread

MAKES 2 LOAVES

 1 cup milk (soy or dairy)
 1/2 cup oil
 1/2 cup dark honey
 1/2 teaspoon salt
 4 cups whole wheat flour
 4 cups unbleached white flour
 1 tablespoon dried yeast

Scald the milk in a saucepan. Add the oil, honey, and salt, stirring well to dissolve the honey. Allow to cool until lukewarm. Sift the whole wheat flour, white flour, and yeast into a large bowl, sifting at least twice to blend the flours evenly. Slowly add the lukewarm milk mixture to the flour, blending until a smooth dough is formed.

On a well floured board, knead the dough for 8 to 10 minutes until it has a light, smooth texture. Place in a wooden bowl, cover, and allow to rise until doubled in bulk.

Punch down the dough, return to the floured board, and knead once again lightly. Shape the dough into two loaves and place in lightly oiled 9-inch loaf pans. Cover and allow to rise again until bulk doubles.

Preheat oven to 375°. Bake for 50 to 60 minutes until nicely browned. Serve hot with honey.

Tomato Bread

MAKES 2 LOAVES

 2 cups tomato paste
 1/2 cup water
 2 tablespoons vegetable oil
 4 tablespoons honey
 1/2 teaspoon sea salt
 1 cake dry yeast, crumbled
 1/4 cup warm water
 6 cups whole wheat flour

Combine the tomato paste and water in a large bowl; add the next three ingredients, mixing thoroughly. Mix yeast with the warm water, stirring until dissolved, and add to the tomato mixture. Gradually add the flour, beating well after each addition until a dough forms that does not stick to the sides of the bowl.

Turn the dough out onto a lightly floured board and knead for 8 minutes or until it attains an elastic texture. Coat a large mixing bowl with oil. Place the dough in the bowl, turning it until evenly coated with oil. Cover with a cloth and allow the dough to rise in a warm place (80°) until it has doubled in size.

Punch down the dough and divide into two loaves; cover, and allow to stand for 10 minutes. Place the loaves in 9-inch loaf pans, cover with a cloth, and allow to rise for 1 hour.

Preheat oven to 350°. Bake the bread for 40–45 minutes, or until a knife inserted into the center of the bread comes out clean. For faster baking, preheat oven to 425° and bake for 25 minutes.

Whole Wheat Bread

MAKES 2 LOAVES

    2 cups warm milk (soy or dairy)
    1/3 cup honey
    1/4 cup sesame oil
    1 teaspoon sea salt (optional)
    2 packages active dry yeast
    1/4 cup lukewarm water
    Approximately 6 cups whole wheat flour

Warm the milk in a saucepan then pour into a mixing bowl. Add the honey, oil, and salt, mixing well. Combine the yeast and water in a bowl and blend well; stir into the milk and honey mixture. Now add the flour a little at a time, working the mixture into a dough.

Turn the dough onto a lightly floured board. Coat fingers with oil and knead for about 10 to 15 minutes until the dough is elastic and smooth. Place the dough in a bowl coated with oil, and rotate the dough until evenly coated with oil. Cover the bowl with a cloth; place in a warm area (80°), and allow the dough to rise for 50 minutes, or until it has doubled in bulk.

Punch down the dough, return it to the floured board, and knead once again lightly. Divide the dough into two 9-inch loaf pans and allow to rise until doubled in bulk.

Preheat oven to 350°. Bake for 40 to 45 minutes, until a knife inserted into the center of the loaf comes out clean. Remove bread from pans and cool on a rack.

Breads and Muffins 47

Seed Bread

MAKES 2 LOAVES

2 cups water
2 tablespoons orange rind, grated
1/2 cup honey
2 teaspoons caraway seed
1 teaspoon anise seeds
1 teaspoon fennel seeds
1 teaspoon sesame seeds
2 tablespoons shortening (preferably soy margarine)
2 packages active dry yeast
1/4 cup lukewarm water
1 cup rye flour, sifted
4 cups whole wheat flour, sifted
1/2 teaspoon sea salt (optional)

Combine the first 7 ingredients in a large pan and bring to a boil; reduce heat and simmer for 5 minutes. Remove pan from the heat and allow the mixture to cool. Soften the yeast in 1/4 cup water and add to the cooled seed mixture. Stir in the rye flour, whole wheat flour, and salt, mixing until a dough is formed; turn onto a lightly floured board. Coat fingers with oil and knead for 10 to 15 minutes until the dough is smooth and elastic. Cover the bowl with a cloth and place in a warm area (80°), allowing the dough to rise until it has doubled in bulk.

Punch down the dough, return it to the floured board, and knead it once again lightly. Now divide the dough in half and shape into 2 loaves. Place each loaf into a 9-inch loaf pan, and allow loaves to rise until they have doubled in bulk.

Preheat oven to 350°. Place the loaves in the oven and bake for 60 minutes, or until brown and a knife inserted into the center of the loaf comes out clean.

You will catch more flies with a spoonful of honey than with a gallon of vinegar.

—English proverb

Quick Breads

Honey enhances the flavor of quick breads and helps retain their freshness. Baked breads will stay fresh for 2 weeks when wrapped properly and stored in the refrigerator. If you plan to freeze the loaves (quick breads freeze especially well), allow them to cool overnight, then slice and wrap the loaves in foil before placing in the freezer. Individual slices are easily removed from a frozen loaf and will defrost quickly.

Honey Carob Loaf

MAKES 1 LOAF

2 tablespoons sesame oil
1 cup honey
2 cups whole wheat flour, sifted
2 teaspoons baking powder
1 teaspoon baking soda
Sea salt to taste
1 egg
1 tablespoon orange rind, grated
1/2 cup carob powder

Preheat oven to 325°. Combine the oil and honey in a mixing bowl. Sift the next 4 ingredients together and gradually add to the oil and honey, mixing well. Beat the egg until light and add to the batter; then stir in the orange rind and half of the carob powder.

Pour the batter into a greased 9-inch loaf pan, and sprinkle the remaining carob powder over the top. Bake for 70 minutes or until a knife inserted into the center of the loaf comes out clean.

Breads and Muffins **49**

Gingerbread

MAKES 1 LOAF

2 1/2 cups unbleached white flour
1 1/2 teaspoons baking soda
1 teaspoon ginger
1 teaspoon cinnamon
1/2 teaspoon sea salt
1/2 cup vegetable oil
1 1/2 cups honey
1/2 cup buttermilk
1 tablespoon orange rind, powdered

Preheat oven to 350°. Sift the flour, soda, ginger, cinnamon, and salt together into a large mixing bowl. Combine the oil and honey in a small bowl; add to the dry ingredients, mixing well. Stir in the buttermilk and orange rind and allow the mixture to stand for 10 minutes. Pour the batter into a 9 x 9 1/2–inch baking pan and bake for 35 minutes.

Peanut Bread

MAKES 1 LOAF

2 cups whole wheat flour
2 teaspoons baking powder
1/2 teaspoon sea salt
1 cup homemade peanut butter
1 cup honey
1 cup milk
2 tablespoons vegetable oil
1/2 cup peanuts, chopped

Preheat oven to 350°. Combine the flour, baking powder, salt, and peanut butter in a large bowl; blend the honey, milk, oil, and peanuts together in another bowl and slowly add to the flour mixture, blending well. Pour into a greased 9–inch loaf pan.

Bake for 60 minutes, or until a knife inserted into the middle of the loaf comes out clean. Cool before slicing.

Variation: To make Honey Tahini Bread, substitute the peanut butter and peanuts with the same amounts of tahini and sesame seeds.

Honey Orange Bread

MAKES 1 LOAF

3 cups white unbleached flour
1 teaspoon baking soda
1/2 teaspoon sea salt
2 tablespoons orange rind
1 cup honey
2 tablespoons sesame oil
1/2 cup fresh orange juice
3/4 cup nuts, chopped
1 egg yolk

Combine the first 4 ingredients in a large bowl. Blend the honey, oil, and orange juice together in another bowl; gradually add to the dry ingredients until an elastic dough is formed. Add the nuts and stir until evenly distributed. Shape the dough in a ball, wrap in a damp cloth, and allow to stand in a cool place for 30 minutes.

Preheat oven to 325°. Place the dough in a lightly oiled 9–inch loaf pan. Beat the egg yolk and brush over the top of the loaf. Bake for approximately 65 minutes, or until a knife inserted into the center of the bread comes out clean. Delicious served warm with orange marmalade.

Honey Nut Bread

MAKES 1 LOAF

2 1/2 cups unbleached white flour, sifted
1 teaspoon baking soda
Sea salt to taste
1 cup honey
2 tablespoons sesame oil
1 cup yogurt
2/3 cup nuts, chopped
2/3 cup raisins, soaked in water for 15 minutes
1 tablespoon orange peel, chopped

Preheat oven to 350°. Sift the first 3 ingredients together into a bowl. Combine the honey and oil in a large mixing bowl. Alternately add the flour mixture and the yogurt to the honey and oil, beating until smooth after each addition. Add the remaining ingredients, blending gently.

Pour the batter into a greased 9–inch loaf pan and bake for 90 minutes, or until a knife inserted into the center of the bread comes out clean.

Millet Bread

MAKES 1 LOAF

1 1/2 cups water
2 cups millet flour
2 teaspoons baking powder
1 teaspoon baking soda
1 cup carrots, grated
1 teaspoon kelp
1 tablespoon honey
1/4 cup sesame oil
2 tablespoons cold water
2 eggs, separated
1 teaspoon sesame oil
1/2 cup sesame seeds

Preheat oven to 350°. Bring the water to a boil in a deep pan; reduce heat and allow to simmer. Sift together the flour, baking powder, and baking soda and add in a slow stream to the water, stirring constantly with a wooden spoon until smooth. Stir in the next 4 ingredients, mixing well, then remove from the stove.

Place the 2 tablespoons cold water in a small bowl; add egg yolks and beat with a whisk. In another bowl, beat the egg whites until stiff peaks form. Gradually add the egg yolks to the flour batter, blending well; gently fold in the egg whites.

Coat an 8-inch baking pan with oil, warm it in the oven, then pour the batter into the pan and top with a sprinkling of sesame seeds. Bake for 45–50 minutes. Allow the bread to cool before slicing.

Honey Apple Bread

MAKES 1 LOAF

1/2 cup vegetable oil
1 cup honey
2 eggs
2 tablespoons fresh lemon juice
1 cup apples, peeled and grated
2 cups unbleached white flour, sifted
2 teaspoons baking powder
1/4 teaspoon baking soda
1 teaspoon sea salt (optional)
1 teaspoon cinnamon

Preheat oven to 350°. Grease a 9-inch loaf pan, line it with waxed paper, and coat the paper with a small amount of oil. Place the oil in a large mixing bowl; add the honey in a fine stream, beating to a creamy texture. Add 1 egg at a time, beating until the mixture is smooth. In another bowl, combine the lemon juice and grated apples, then add to the honey mixture.

Sift together the flour, baking powder, baking soda, salt, and cinnamon; add a small amount at a time to the honey mixture, beating well after each addition. Pour the batter into the pan and allow it to stand for 30 minutes.

Bake for 60 minutes, or until a knife inserted into the center of the loaf comes out clean. Cool before serving.

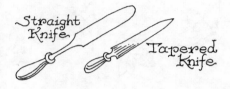

Spatula

Curved Knife

Wax Knife

Whole Wheat Banana Bread

MAKES 1 LOAF

1/3 cup honey
1/2 cup sesame oil
3 medium bananas, mashed
2 eggs
1 teaspoon vanilla
1 cup milk
1/2 cup wheat germ
2 teaspoons baking powder
1 teaspoon baking soda
1/2 teaspoon salt
1/2 teaspoon cinnamon
1 1/2 cups whole wheat flour
1/2 cup nuts

Preheat oven to 325°. Mix the honey and oil together in a large mixing bowl. Add the mashed bananas, eggs, and vanilla. Combine the rest of the ingredients, except the nuts, in a separate bowl and add to the banana mixture, blending lightly; then gently fold in the nuts.

Pour the mixture into an oiled 9–inch loaf pan. Bake for 65 minutes or until a knife inserted into the middle of the loaf comes out clean.

Hive with handle for retreiving a Swarm

Fruit and Nut Bread

MAKES 1 LOAF

1/4 cup unbleached white flour
1/2 teaspoon sea salt
1 teaspoon baking soda
1 cup whole wheat flour
2/3 cup mild-flavored honey
1 cup buttermilk
2 well beaten eggs (optional)
2 tablespoons vegetable oil
1/2 cup seedless raisins
1/2 cup diced dry apricots (or other dried fruits)
1 cup walnuts (or other nuts), finely chopped
1 teaspoon lemon rind (optional)

Sift the white flour together with the salt and baking soda into a large bowl; then add the whole wheat flour. Combine the honey, buttermilk, eggs, and oil in a separate bowl; add to the dry ingredients, mixing thoroughly. Now add the fruit, nuts, and lemon rind. Allow the batter to stand overnight.

Preheat oven to 350°. Pour the batter into a greased 8–inch loaf pan and bake for 60 minutes, or until a knife inserted into the middle of the loaf comes out clean. Place on a wire rack for 10 minutes before removing the loaf from the pan. Allow to cool before serving.

Breads and Muffins 55

Bran Muffins

1 cup whole bran
1 cup boiling water
1/2 cup homemade nut butter
1 cup honey
1 egg
2 1/2 cups unbleached white flour
2 1/2 teaspoons baking soda
1/2 teaspoon sea salt
2 cups buttermilk
1/4 cup wheat germ

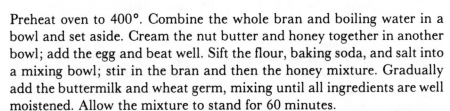

Preheat oven to 400°. Combine the whole bran and boiling water in a bowl and set aside. Cream the nut butter and honey together in another bowl; add the egg and beat well. Sift the flour, baking soda, and salt into a mixing bowl; stir in the bran and then the honey mixture. Gradually add the buttermilk and wheat germ, mixing until all ingredients are well moistened. Allow the mixture to stand for 60 minutes.

Grease 18 muffin cups and fill each cup 2/3 full with batter. Bake for 20 minutes or until brown.

Nut Butter Muffins

2 cups of any gluten flour, sifted
1/4 tablespoon mace
1/2 teaspoon sea salt
1 1/2 teaspoons baking powder
1 teaspoon baking soda
1 cup oatmeal, uncooked
1/3 cup honey
3/4 cup milk
1/3 cup homemade nut butter
1 egg, beaten
1/4 cup vegetable oil

Preheat oven to 400°. Sift together the first 5 ingredients; combine the remaining ingredients, except the oatmeal, in a large bowl. Gradually add the sifted flour mixture, then the oatmeal to the liquid mixture. Mix until well moistened. Grease 12 muffin cups and fill each cup 2/3 full with batter. Bake for 20 minutes or until brown.

Variation: Mix 1/2 cup of dried fruits or fresh berries into the batter before pouring into the muffin cups.

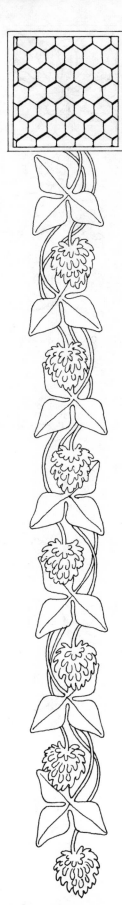

Yahweh alone is his guide,
with him is no alien god.
He gives him the heights of the land to ride,
he feeds him on the yield of the mountains,
he gives him honey from the rock to taste.
                                        —Deuteronomy

Soups

Fruit soups, a part of the traditional cuisine of Germany, are soups for all seasons. They can be served piping hot or chilled, providing quick energy and old-fashioned goodness.

Chestnut Soup (*Soupe de Castagne*)

SERVES 4

Honey chestnut soup is very popular in Auvergne, France where chestnuts grow in abundance. Prepared with cow's milk or goat's milk, this soup is standard winter fare for family meals.

Note: Raw chestnuts will not keep at room temperature but will keep several months if placed in a ventilated plastic bag and stored in the refrigerator.

    2 cups water
    24 chestnuts
    4 cups milk
    1 cup water
    1/4 cup honey
    1 celery stalk, chopped
    1 teaspoon salt
    4 slices toasted Honey Nut Bread,
        whole wheat bread, or cornbread

Bring the water to a vigorous boil in a large pan; slit the chestnuts, then drop them into the boiling water for 5 minutes. Pour off the water and shell the nuts. Place the nutmeats in a large bowl and crumble with a fork until the texture is like a coarse purée.

In a large pan, bring the milk, 1 cup water, honey, celery, and salt to a boil; add the chestnuts, reduce heat, and simmer for 30 minutes. Place one slice of toasted bread into each individual serving bowl. Pour the soup and serve piping hot.

Variation: Pour the soup into individual earthenware soup bowls, sprinkle with cheese, and place under the broiler until the cheese melts.

Milk soups also can be made with 1 cup of barley, oats, or millet instead of chestnuts.

Spinach Soup

SERVES 5

> 1 cup water
> 1/2 cup chicken stock
> 10 ounces fresh leaf spinach
> 16 ounces plain yogurt
> 1/2 cup wheat germ
> 2 tablespoons honey
> 1 tablespoon chopped chives
> 1/2 teaspoon celery salt

Place the water, chicken stock, and spinach in a blender and blend at low speed until smooth. Add the remaining ingredients and blend thoroughly at high speed. Pour into a serving dish or individual soup cups and refrigerate for 1 hour before serving.

Split Pea Soup

SERVES 6

> 4 1/2 quarts water
> 1 pound split peas
> 2 tablespoons oil
> 1 carrot, diced
> 1 onion, thinly sliced
> 1 leek, thinly sliced
> 2 tablespoons honey
> A dash of pepper

Soak the split peas in two quarts of water for three or four hours; drain the peas and rinse in cold water. Combine the peas and the remaining 2 1/2 quarts fresh water in a large pan, and bring to a boil; reduce heat and simmer gently.

Place the oil, carrot, onion, and leek in a skillet; sauté for 4 or 5 minutes, then add to the peas. Continue simmering for 60 minutes or until the peas are soft.

When the peas are done, add the honey and pour into a blender; blend at low speed until smooth. Pour into a soup tureen or individual serving bowls. Serve with a dash of pepper, if desired.

Variation: This hearty soup can be made with lentils (60 minutes cooking

time), chickpeas (4 hours cooking time), or kidney beans (2 hours cooking time).

Corsican Turnip Soup

SERVES 4 TO 6

12 turnips (medium size), thinly sliced
1 1/2 tablespoons vegetable oil
2 cups water
1 quart milk
2 tablespoons honey
A dash of grated nutmeg
Salt and pepper to taste
6 slices of whole wheat bread

Heat the oil in a heavy skillet. Add the thinly sliced turnips and sauté for 4 to 5 minutes. Add the water and bring to a boil; cover and simmer for about 10 minutes, or until turnips are transparent. Pour the water and turnips into a blender and blend until smooth. Now turn the mixture into a large pan and slowly stir in the milk and honey; add the nutmeg, salt, and pepper. Bring to a boil, reduce heat, and simmer for 4 to 5 minutes. Place the bread slices in a soup-tureen, pour in the soup, and serve immediately.

Variation: This soup also can be made with carrots, Swedish turnips, pumpkin, or rutabagas. If 1 cup barley is added, it becomes a meal in itself, perfect for cold weather.

Sweet and Sour Corn Soup

SERVES 4 TO 5

4 cups chicken stock
2 cups corn kernels, cooked
1 tablespoon unbleached white flour
1 tablespoon honey
2 tablespoons cider vinegar
1 tablespoon natural soy sauce (shoyu)
1 scallion, minced

Bring the stock to a boil, then add the corn. Reduce heat and simmer for 3 minutes. Stir in the flour and the remaining ingredients and simmer for 5 minutes more. Serve hot.

Smoker

Simple Extractor

Straight Knife

Tapered Knife

Spatula

Curved Knife

Wax Knife

Hive with handle for retreiving a Swarm

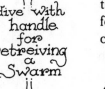

Vegetable Soup

SERVES 4

2 leeks
4 carrots
1 onion
1 small turnip
2 celery stalks
6 cups water
2 tablespoons vegetable oil
3 tablespoons whole wheat flour
1 tablespoon prepared mustard
3 tablespoons honey
1 teaspoon sweet basil
1/2 teaspoon cumin
1/2 teaspoon parsley

Dice all the vegetables and place in a medium-sized pan. Add the water and bring to a boil, then reduce heat and simmer for 20 minutes. Retain the cooking water.

In a separate pan, heat the oil over medium heat and gradually add the flour, mustard, and honey, stirring constantly with a wooden spoon for 3 minutes. Now, slowly stir in 4 cups of the reserved water, the cooked vegetables, and herbs; simmer for 10 minutes. Serve piping hot.

Apple Soup

SERVES 4 TO 5

2 cups applesauce
1/4 cup honey
2 cups loganberry or cranberry juice
1/4 cup lemon juice
Salt (vegetable salt preferred) to taste
White wine (optional)
1 tablespoon grated lemon peel

Combine the first 5 ingredients in a pan and simmer over low heat stirring constantly for 6 to 8 minutes or until clear. Pour into soup cups or bowls and refrigerate for 1 hour. Just before serving, add 1 teaspoon of wine to each serving and sprinkle with grated lemon peel.

Berry Soup

SERVES 8

4 cups of any berries in season
2 cups water
1 cup apple juice
1/2 cup honey
A sprinkling of nutmeg
A dash of vegetable salt
1/4 cup lemon juice
1 tablespoon chopped mint

Combine the water and berries in a saucepan and bring to a boil; cover, and simmer until the berries are soft. Now pour into a blender, and add the apple juice, honey, nutmeg, salt, and lemon juice; blend until smooth. Pour into cups and sprinkle with chopped mint. Serve hot, or refrigerate for one hour before serving.

Tutti-Frutti Soup

SERVES 4

1 stick cinnamon
1/2 cup water
3 cups fruit juice (orange or pineapple)
1 cup cranberry sauce
Sea salt and pepper to taste
2 tablespoons tapioca
1/4 cup honey

Simmer the cinnamon in the water for 5 minutes. Add the fruit juice, cranberry sauce, salt, and pepper, and bring to a boil; reduce heat to a simmer. Gradually stir in the tapioca; add the honey and continue simmering for 5 minutes more. Pour into individual serving bowls and refrigerate for 1 hour. Serve chilled, with a twist of lemon.

Soups 63

Rhubarb Soup

SERVES 4

> 1 pound rhubarb
> 6 cups water
> 1 cup yogurt
> 1/4 cup honey
> 2 tablespoons thinly sliced leek or scallion
>   greens (optional)

Combine the water and rhubarb in a medium-sized pan and cook for 20 to 25 minutes until soft. Drain the rhubarb (saving the cooking water) and place in a blender; add 4 cups of cooking water, yogurt, and honey; blend at low speed until smooth. If desired, serve garnished with a sprinkling of thin leek slices or scallion greens.

Sunflower Seed Soup

SERVES 4

> 6 cups chicken stock
> 1/4 cup chives, chopped
> 1 teaspoon sweet basil, chopped
> 2 cups sunflower seeds, shelled
> 1 tablespoon honey
> Sea salt to taste

Combine the chicken stock with the remaining ingredients in a medium-sized pan and bring to a boil. Reduce heat and simmer for 40 minutes. Serve hot.

. . . more desirable than gold,
even that the finest gold;
his words are sweeter than honey,
even that honey that drips from the comb.
  —Psalm 19

Salad Dressings,
Sauces, Pickles and Relishes

Homemade dressings, sauces, and relishes add a festive touch to the simplest meal. The use of honey adds a unique flavor to green salads or a medley of fresh fruits. In addition, the fruits stay bright and fresh-looking for hours when refrigerated.

Honey Vinegar

MAKES 1 GALLON

Honey vinegar should be made in an unwashed, wooden barrel. Glazed or metal containers must not be used; the acid in vinegar will react and the vinegar will become poisonous.

  1 mother of vinegar (obtained from a winery)
    or 1 cake active dry yeast
  1/4 cup wine vinegar
  2 pounds honey
  1 gallon water (soft or rain water)

Combine mother of vinegar and the wine in a wooden barrel; add the honey and water, filling the barrel no more than 3 parts full; mix well. Place the barrel in a warm area outdoors in an open shed; the temperature should be 70°–80°. Leave the bung-hole of the barrel open, but cover it with muslin or gauze to keep insects out. Allow the barrel to stand for 6 to 8 weeks.

When the liquid has fermented, strain the vinegar into another wooden barrel; allow it to stand for two weeks, then strain, and pour into sterilized bottles. When the sediment settles to the bottom of the bottles, decant the vinegar into fresh bottles.

Leave the mother of vinegar in the barrel and immediately add a fresh supply of honey and water.

Honey Yogurt Dressing, No. 1

MAKES 2 CUPS

1 egg yolk
1/2 cup honey
1 cup yogurt
1/2 cup lemon juice

Beat the yolk in the top of a double boiler, add the honey, and place the double-boiler over low heat for 3 to 4 minutes. Remove from heat and place the top of the double boiler in cold water until the egg yolk is cool. Add the yogurt and lemon juice, mixing well. Pour into a container and store in the refrigerator.

Honey Yogurt Dressing, No. 2

MAKES 1 1/2 CUPS

1 cup yogurt
2 tablespoons fresh lemon juice
1/4 cup honey (clover or orange blossom honey)
A dash of vegetable salt
A dash of Tabasco (optional)
1 teaspoon coriander
1 teaspoon powdered orange peel

Combine the ingredients in a blender at low speed until the mixture has a smooth texture. Refrigerate at least one hour. Serve over green salad or fruit salad.

Honey Kefir Dressing

MAKES 2 1/2 CUPS

2 cups kefir
1/2 cup honey
1 tablespoon cinnamon

Combine the ingredients in a blender at low speed until smooth and creamy. Refrigerate at least one hour. Serve over green salad or fruit salad.

Honey Cider Vinegar Dressing

MAKES 2 CUPS

1 cup cottage cheese
1/3 cup cider vinegar
1/4 cup sesame oil
1/4 cup honey
1/4 teaspoon paprika
1/2 teaspoon sea salt

Combine the ingredients in a blender at high speed until smooth and creamy. Pour into a container and store in the refrigerator. Serve over green salads and vegetables.

Honey Mint Dressing

MAKES 1 1/2 CUPS

1/2 cup honey
1/2 cup water
1/2 teaspoon ground cardamom
1 teaspoon fresh mint leaves, crushed
1 lemon rind, grated
1/4 cup fresh lemon juice
1/4 cup sesame oil

Combine the honey, water, and cardamom in a saucepan; bring to a boil, reduce heat, and simmer for 3 minutes. Turn off the heat, add the mint leaves, and allow the mixture to cool 10 to 15 minutes. Pour the liquid from the pan through a strainer into a blender; add the lemon juice and oil and blend at low speed until smooth. Pour into a container, and store in the refrigerator. Shake well before serving with greens, vegetables, or fruit salads.

Honey Lemon Dressing

MAKES 1 CUP

Honey lemon dressing is a Mediterranean dressing that will not spoil. It prevents fresh fruits, particularly avocados, from turning brown.

1/2 cup honey
1/2 cup lemon juice
1/2 teaspoon paprika
A dash of sea salt

Combine the ingredients in a blender and mix at low speed until smooth. Pour into a container and place in the refrigerator. Serve over cottage cheese, sliced oranges, sliced bananas, sliced pineapple, or use as a dressing for green salads.
Variation: For a spicier taste, use red pepper in place of paprika and allow the dressing to stand in the container for 24 hours.

Honey Avocado Dressing

MAKES 2 CUPS

1/2 cup clover honey
1 large ripe avocado
1 cup kefir or yogurt
1 teaspoon fresh orange peel, grated

Place the avocado in a medium-sized bowl and mash well with a wooden fork; add the honey to the avocado, blending well with the fork. Add the kefir or yogurt and orange peel; mix well. Refrigerate at least one hour. Serve over berries, fresh pineapple, or ripe bananas.

Smoker
Simple Extractor

Straight Knife
Tapered Knife

Spatula

Curved Knife

Wax Knife

Honey French Dressing

MAKES 3 CUPS

1 cup vegetable oil (olive or sesame*)
1/4 cup tomato juice
1/3 cup vinegar
1/3 cup honey
1 teaspoon onion, grated
1 garlic clove, halved
1 teaspoon sea salt
1 teaspoon paprika

Combine the ingredients in a blender at low speed for 1 minute. Pour into a container and store in the refrigerator. Use over green salads, cold green asparagus, or broccoli.

* Sesame oil gives the dressing a nutty flavor.

Hive with handle for retrieving a Swarm

Honey Lemon-Pineapple Sauce

MAKES 1 1/2 CUPS

1/2 cup honey
1/2 cup fresh pineapple juice
1/2 cup fresh lemon juice

Mix the ingredients well by hand or in a blender at low speed; chill. Serve over a fruit salad or pour over rice with a dash of cinnamon.

Honey Lime Sauce

MAKES 1 1/2 CUPS

1 tablespoon whole wheat flour
1/4 cup fresh lime juice
1 cup honey
1 teaspoon grated lime peel

Combine the flour and lime juice in a saucepan. Slowly add the honey and place over low heat, cooking until the mixture thickens; stir in the lime peel. Serve hot over rice and pastries, or chill and serve over salads and fruits.

Honey Yogurt Sauce

MAKES 2 1/2 CUPS

1/2 cup honey
2 cups yogurt
1 tablespoon cinnamon

Place all the ingredients in a blender at low speed for 1 minute. Chill for at least 30 minutes. Serve over fruit salads, or use as a dip with cookies.

Honey Rose Sauce

MAKES 2 CUPS

This dressing is used over rice puddings in the Middle East.

1 cup orange blossom honey
1 cup kefir
2 tablespoons butter
1/4 cup rosewater

Melt the butter in a double-boiler and add the honey and kefir; simmer for 15 minutes, stirring occasionally with a wooden spoon. Stir in the rosewater with a wire whisk and simmer for 3 minutes more. Remove from heat and serve hot over dumplings or rice.

Honey Sweet and Sour Sauce

MAKES 2 CUPS

1/8 cup vegetable oil
1/8 cup flour
2 cups chicken stock
2 tablespoons honey
2 tablespoons hot mustard
1 1/2 tablespoons natural soy sauce (shoyu)

Heat the vegetable oil in a skillet over medium heat. Reduce heat and stir in the flour with a wooden spoon; gradually add the broth, stirring constantly to avoid lumps. Add the honey, mustard, and soy sauce; simmer for 4 to 5 minutes. Serve hot with chicken.

Honey Ravigote Sauce

MAKES 2 CUPS

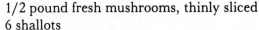

2 tablespoons vegetable oil
1/2 pound fresh mushrooms, thinly sliced
6 shallots
1/4 cup wine vinegar
1/4 cup garlic stock
2 tablespoons honey
2 ounces raisins
2 ounces chopped almonds
1/4 teaspoon nutmeg
Sea salt to taste
3 ounces cream cheese

Heat the oil in a heavy skillet over medium heat; add the mushrooms and shallots, and sauté until brown. Reduce heat and stir in the rest of the ingredients, except the cheese, mixing well. Add the cheese in pieces, stirring constantly with a wooden spoon for 2 minutes. Remove from the heat and serve over chicken or boiled white fish, or pour over a bed of boiled and diced potatoes.

Honey Mustard Sauce

MAKES 2 CUPS

1/4 cup hot mustard (or 1 tablespoon dry mustard
   in 1/2 cup water)
1 tablespoon flour
1 cup chicken stock
2 egg yolks
A dash of sea salt
1/2 cup honey

Combine the hot mustard and flour in a wooden bowl; gradually add the chicken stock, beating slowly with a whisk. Beat the egg yolks with the salt in a small cup until pale and creamy; add to the stock mixture, stirring constantly. Add the honey and mix well. Use as a condiment or serve warm with poultry.

Honey Paprika Sauce

MAKES 2 CUPS

    1 tablespoon vegetable oil
    2 onions very thinly sliced
    1 cup milk stock
    1/4 cup honey
    1/2 cup tahini
    1 tablespoon paprika
    Celery salt to taste

Heat the oil in a skillet over medium heat; add the onions and sauté until they become translucent and form a paste. Stir in the rest of the ingredients with a wooden spoon; reduce heat and simmer for 5 minutes. Serve with any white fish.

Crab-Apple Pickle

MAKES 2 TO 3 CUPS

    2 cups honey
    1 cup vinegar
    2 cinnamon sticks
    6 whole cloves
    2 to 3 cups whole crab-apples

Combine the first 4 ingredients in a saucepan; bring to a boil, then reduce heat and simmer. Gently drop a portion of the crab-apples, one by one, into the simmering syrup; cook until apples are translucent. Carefully remove the apples from the pan with a mesh skimmer and place in a bowl to cool; repeat the process with the remaining apples.

Fill 8 ounce sterilized jars 3/4 full with the apples; remove the whole spices from the syrup and pour over the apples. Store in the refrigerator.

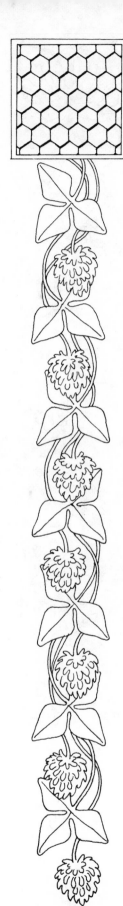

Cucumber Pickle

MAKES 2 CUPS

1/2 cup cider vinegar
1 cup honey
2 tablespoons corn or sesame oil
1/2 teaspoon sea salt
A sprinkling of pepper
2 small cucumbers, unpeeled and thinly
    sliced in rounds
1 small onion, thinly sliced
1 teaspoon parsley, minced

Combine the first 5 ingredients in a saucepan over low heat; stir until the mixture is smooth. Remove from heat. Combine the cucumbers and onion in a heat-proof dish with a cover; pour in the hot sauce and sprinkle parsley over the top. Allow to cool, then cover, and refrigerate overnight before serving.

Pickled Mushrooms

MAKES 1 1/2 CUPS

1 cup honey
1/2 cup cider vinegar or white wine vinegar
2 tablespoons vegetable oil
1 small pimento, crushed
1 teaspoon oregano
1/2 teaspoon sea salt
1 pound small mushrooms, washed
1 medium-sized white onion, thinly sliced

Combine the first 6 ingredients in a saucepan and simmer over low heat; stir for 4 to 5 minutes until mixture is smooth, then remove from heat. Combine the mushrooms and onion slices in a heat-proof dish with a lid; pour in the hot sauce. Allow to cool, then cover, and refrigerate a minimum of 6 hours.

Corn Relish

MAKES 3 CUPS

    3 cups fresh or frozen whole kernel corn
    2 cups honey
    1 cup vinegar
    2 tablespoons sesame oil
    1 teaspoon dry mustard
    A dash of sea salt
    1 sweet red pepper, thinly sliced and diced
    1 small white onion, minced

Place the corn in a saucepan with water to cover, and bring to a boil. Cover, reduce to a medium heat, and allow the corn to boil for 10 minutes. Drain off the water. Combine the next 5 ingredients in a saucepan over low heat until warm; do not boil. Combine the corn, red pepper, and onion in a large heat-proof dish with a lid; pour the warm sauce over the vegetables and mix well. Cover and refrigerate overnight before serving.

Variation: The corn can be substituted with shallots, cauliflower, gherkins, carrots, or with a medley of chopped vegetables in the same proportions.

Cranberry Relish

MAKES 3 1/2 CUPS

    2 cups raw cranberries
    1 cup celery
    A dash of sea salt
    1/2 cup to 1 cup honey
    1/2 cup fresh lemon juice

Place the cranberries and the celery in a bowl; sprinkle with sea salt. Blend the honey and lemon juice in another bowl and pour over the cranberry mixture. Cover, and allow to stand overnight.

The Owl and the Pussy-cat went to sea
* In a beautiful pea-green boat,*
They took some honey, and plenty of money,
* Wrapped up in a five-pound note.*
    —Edward Lear, "The Owl and the Pussy-Cat"

Salads

Salmon Salad

SERVES 4

4 cups water
1 pound fresh red salmon
1/2 teaspoon fennel seeds
1/2 teaspoon mixed Italian seasoning herbs
1 tablespoon cider or white wine vinegar
1 cup celery, chopped
1/4 cup green onions, sliced (approximately
   2 onions)
1 small cucumber, thinly sliced
2 cups soybean sprouts
1/2 cup Yogurt Salad Dressing, No. 1 or
   Honey French Dressing
1 teaspoon capers or parsley sprigs

Combine the first 5 ingredients in a pan and bring to a boil; reduce heat and simmer for 20 to 25 minutes, or until the salmon flakes. Pour off the liquid and set the salmon aside.

Combine the celery, onions, cucumber, and sprouts in a salad bowl; using a fork, flake the salmon into the bowl and lightly toss the ingredients together. Top with one of the dressings and garnish with a sprinkling of capers or parsley sprigs.

Variation: Substitute the salmon with turbot, filet of sole, or cod.

Peanut Chicken Salad

SERVES 4 TO 6

1 head lettuce
4 cups cooked chicken, diced
1 cup seedless green grapes, halved
1 cup celery, diced
1/4 cup honey
1 cup natural yogurt
1 cup peanuts, shelled and chopped
1 teaspoon hot mustard
Sea salt to taste

Arrange a bed of lettuce leaves in a salad bowl. Combine the remaining ingredients in a large bowl, stirring until blended. Spoon over the lettuce leaves and serve.

Smoker

Simple Extractor

Straight Knife

Tapered Knife

Spatula

Curved Knife

Wax Knife

Hive with handle for retreiving a Swarm

Green Pea Salad

SERVES 4

1 cup fresh green peas
2 cups water
1 cup carrots, grated
1/2 cup cooked beets, diced
1 cup Honey Yogurt Dressing, No. 1

Bring the water to a vigorous boil in a saucepan; add the peas; boil for 5 minutes or until tender. Pour off the water and combine the peas with the carrots and beets in a salad bowl. Add the dressing, and gently mix well.

Beet Salad

SERVES 4

4 beets, peeled, sliced, and cooked
1 head chicory lettuce, shredded
2 apples, peeled and grated
1 onion, chopped
1/4 cup honey
Juice of 1 lemon
1/4 cup sour cream or yogurt
1/2 teaspoon hot mustard
1/2 tablespoon horseradish
A dash of sea salt
1/2 teaspoon coarsely ground black pepper
8 pitted green olives

Place the beets, lettuce, apples, and onion in a salad bowl. Combine the rest of the ingredients, except the olives, in another bowl, mixing well. Pour over the vegetables and garnish with olives.

Spatula

Curved Knife

Wax Knife

Hive with handle for retrieving a Swarm

Goat Cheese Salad

SERVES 4

1 head lettuce
8 ounces of goat cheese or 8 ounces feta cheese
1 cup fresh cherry tomatoes
2 tablespoons vegetable oil
2 tablespoons honey
Juice of 1 lemon
10 pitted black olives
1 teaspoon capers
1/2 teaspoon tarragon
1 tablespoon chopped chives or green onions
Sea salt to taste

Arrange a bed of lettuce leaves in a salad bowl; crumble the cheese over the lettuce and add the tomatoes. Combine the oil, honey, and lemon juice in a small bowl, beating with a fork until well blended. Add the olives (quarter to maximize their fragrance) and the remaining ingredients, mixing well. Pour over the salad and serve.

New Hampshire Cider Slaw

SERVES 6

1 large cabbage, quartered, cored, and shredded
2 medium onions, sliced paper thin
1/2 cup honey
1 tablespoon sea salt
1 teaspoon dry mustard
2/3 cup corn oil
1 cup apple cider vinegar
1 teaspoon celery seed

Place the cabbage in a large bowl; add the onions. Pour in the honey; mix well, coating the cabbage and onions with honey. Combine the remaining ingredients in a small saucepan and bring to a boil over low heat. Pour over the cabbage and onions; toss well and allow the mixture to stand at room temperature for 4 to 5 hours. As the slaw marinates, its volume will reduce by half. This salad will keep two weeks if covered and stored in the refrigerator.

Celery Salad

SERVES 2 TO 3

4 stalks celery, diced
2 green sweet peppers, thinly sliced
1 bunch watercress, shredded
4 carrots, thinly sliced
1/2 cup chopped nuts
1 cup Yogurt Salad Dressing, No. 1

Combine the first 5 ingredients in a salad bowl. Add the dressing and toss lightly.

Shredded Cabbage Salad

SERVES 2 TO 3

1 small head cabbage, shredded
1 red pepper, blanched, and thinly sliced
1 cup carrots, thinly sliced
1/4 cup pinenuts
1 cup Honey Cider Vinegar Dressing

Combine the first 4 ingredients in a salad bowl. Add dressing and toss lightly.

Cauliflower Salad

SERVES 2 TO 3

1 small head cauliflower, raw or cooked
1 cup Yogurt Salad Dressing, No. 1 or Honey
   Lemon Dressing
1/2 cup walnuts, chopped

Pull or cut the cauliflower into bite-sized pieces and place in a salad bowl. Top with one of the dressings and garnish with the walnuts.

Sauerkraut Salad

SERVES 4

1 pound sauerkraut, drained
3 apples, peeled and sliced
1/4 cup sour pickles, sliced
1 onion, very thinly sliced
2 tablespoons dill
1/8 cup honey
Juice of 1 lemon
Sea salt and pepper (optional)
2 tablespoons parsley, shredded

Combine the first 5 ingredients in an earthenware bowl; blend the honey, lemon, salt, and pepper together in a small dish and pour over the sauerkraut mixture. Garnish the salad with a sprinkling of parsley.

Florissant Salad

SERVES 4

1/2 cup raisins
1 cup cooked white or brown rice
8 ounces fresh or frozen whole kernel corn, cooked
1/2 teaspoon saffron
3 tablespoons corn oil
Juice of 1 lemon
1 teaspoon hot mustard
2 tablespoons honey
A dash of sesame salt
1 carrot, grated
1 cup soya sprouts
10 walnuts
1 head bib lettuce

Soak the raisins in water or sherry to cover for at least one hour. Cook the rice and the corn. When the rice has finished cooking, add the saffron while it is still warm; mix lightly, and set aside to cool. Drain the corn and set aside.

Combine the oil, lemon, mustard, honey, and salt in a salad bowl. Add the rice, corn, and grated carrot, mixing gently; then add the soya sprouts, walnuts, lettuce, and drained raisins. Toss lightly just before serving.

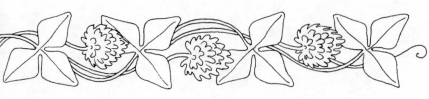

Cucumber Salad

SERVES 4

2 medium-sized cucumbers, peeled and
   thinly sliced
1 cup yogurt
2 tablespoons honey
Crushed garlic (1 to 3 cloves, according to taste)
A dash of tabasco (optional)
2 parsley sprigs

Place the cucumbers in a salad bowl. Combine the yogurt, honey, and crushed garlic in another bowl, mixing well; spoon over the cucumbers. Decorate with parsley sprigs.

Cucumber à La Turk

SERVES 5

2 cups plain natural yogurt
3 tablespoons honey
Juice of 1 lemon
A dash of sea salt
A sprinkling of pepper
1 teaspoon paprika
1 tablespoon chopped mint leaves
3 chilled cucumbers, peeled and thinly sliced

Combine the first five ingredients in a bowl; mix well. Shortly before serving, peel and slice the cucumbers and place in a serving bowl. (If the cucumbers are in season, peeling is not necessary, but do wash the skins thoroughly.) Pour the dressing over the cucumbers; sprinkle with the paprika and mint leaves, and serve.

Spring Salad

SERVES 4

1 cup fresh artichoke hearts, diced
1/2 cup small turnips, shredded
1 cup fresh carrots, shredded
1 cup fresh radishes, sliced
1 cup Honey Pineapple Sauce or Yogurt
    Salad Dressing, No. 1

Combine the first 4 ingredients in a salad bowl and toss lightly. Top with one of the dressings.

Autumn Salad

SERVES 4

1 head lettuce
1 cup carrots, shredded
1/2 cup celery, chopped
1 cup tart apples, peeled and diced
1/4 cup honey
1/2 cup pineapple juice
Juice of 1 lime
1/2 cup walnuts or filberts, chopped

Tear the lettuce into small pieces in a salad bowl. Add the carrots, celery, and apples and toss lightly. Combine honey, pineapple juice, and lime in a blender at low speed until well blended; pour over the salad. Top with the nuts and serve.

Fresh Peach Salad

SERVES 4

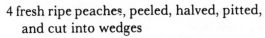

    4 fresh ripe peaches, peeled, halved, pitted,
        and cut into wedges
    1 cup celery
    1/2 cup walnuts, coarsely chopped
    2 tablespoons mild honey (e.g., clover)
    1/2 cup natural yogurt
    Salad greens
    4 fresh whole strawberries

Combine the first 4 ingredients in a large bowl, tossing lightly; refrigerate until ready to use. Immediately before serving, gently fold the yogurt into the salad. Arrange salad greens on individual plates; spoon the fruit mixture over the greens, and garnish with fresh strawberries.

Cantaloupe Salad

SERVES 4

    2 chilled medium cantaloupes, cut into halves
    1/4 cup honey
    1 cup cottage cheese
    1/2 cup berries in season (raspberries, blue-
        berries, strawberries)
    1/4 cup port wine or sweet sherry (optional)

Scoop out the seeds of the cantaloupe halves and place the halves on individual serving dishes. Combine the honey, cottage cheese, and berries in a bowl, mixing lightly with a wooden spoon. Fill the cantaloupe halves with the mixture, and pour 1 teaspoon of wine or sherry over the top of each. Serve immediately.

Honeydew Melon   SERVES 4

1/4 cup water
1/2 cup honey
1/4 cup orange juice
1/4 cup lime juice
1/2 lemon, sliced
30 peanuts, shelled and finely chopped, or
    4 tablespoons homemade peanut butter
1 medium-sized honeydew melon
Approximately 4 cups crushed ice

Add the water to a saucepan and bring to a boil; add the next 5 ingredients, reduce heat, and simmer for 5 minutes, stirring constantly. Remove pan from heat and allow the mixture to cool.

Cut off the top of the melon 2 to 2 1/2 inches from base of stem; set the top aside. Form melon balls by scooping out the honeydew with an ice-cream scoop or spoon. After all the melon has been removed, fill the shell with melon balls and place in a large bowl half filled with crushed ice. Pour the peanut mixture over the melon balls and cover with the melon top. Chill for 30 minutes in the refrigerator before serving.

Banana Salad   SERVES 4

2 bananas, peeled and sliced
4 large mushrooms, sliced
1 apple, peeled and thinly sliced
1 red beet, cooked and diced
1/4 cup raisins
1/4 cup tahini
1 cup yogurt
4 tablespoons honey
1/2 teaspoon dry mustard

Place the bananas, mushrooms, apple, beet, and raisins in a salad bowl; combine the remaining ingredients in another bowl, mixing with a fork. Pour the dressing over the salad mixture and toss lightly before serving.

Smoker
Simple Extractor

Straight Knife
Tapered Knife

Spatula

Curved Knife

Wax Knife

Hive with handle for retreiving a Swarm

Orange Salad

SERVES 4

4 oranges, peeled, and sliced into thin rounds
Juice of 1 lemon
2 tablespoons chopped mint
2 tablespoons orange blossom honey
1/2 cup cottage cheese
A dash of sea salt

Place the orange slices in an hors d'oeuvre dish. Combine the remaining ingredients in a small bowl and pour over the orange slices.
Variation: Substitute the orange slices with fresh apricot sections or avocado slices. Honey will keep the avocados fresh-looking even if the salad is prepared in advance and refrigerated.

Orange–Coconut Salad

SERVES 4

1 cup shredded watercress
1/4 cup honey
4 oranges, peeled and sliced
3/4 cup grated coconut
8 fresh cherries or strawberries, pitted and halved
1/2 cup Honey Lemon Dressing

Arrange the watercress on a serving plate. Warm the honey in a saucepan over low heat; do not boil. Using a fork or thin skewer, dip each orange section into the warm honey, then sprinkle generously with coconut, and place on the watercress; garnish with the cherries or strawberries. Pour Honey Lemon Dressing over the orange slices and serve.

Smoker *Simple Extractor* *Straight Knife* *Tapered Knife*

While Honey lies in Every Flower, no doùbt
It takes a Bee to get the Honey out.
—Guiterman, "A Poet's Proverbs"

Spatula

Curved Knife

Wax Knife

Fish and Fowl

Hive with handle for retreiving a Swarm

Honey White Fish in Marinade

SERVES 4

    1 pound of white fish (sole fillets or flounder)
    2 cups water
    3 cups Uncooked Marinade

Bring the water to a boil in a pan or skillet; reduce heat, add the fish and poach gently for 5 minutes. Drain off the water.

    Cut the fillets into 1 1/2 inch-long pieces. Place the fish in a bowl and cover with Uncooked Marinade; marinate for 3 hours. Pour off the marinade and place the pieces of fish on a serving platter. Serve with steamed potatoes.

Honey Glazed Shrimp

SERVES 4

    1 pound shelled shrimp
    1 cup honey
    1/2 cup bread crumbs
    A dash of curry
    Vegetable oil for deep frying (about 4 cups)
    1/2 cup of Honey Mustard Sauce

Combine the honey, bread crumbs, and curry in a bowl. Dip the shrimp in the honey mixture and coat well. Place the oil in a deep fryer and heat to frying temperature. Drop the coated shrimp into the oil for about 3 minutes, or until golden brown. Drain on paper towels. Serve with Honey Mustard Sauce.

Deviled Crab

SERVES 4

2 tablespoons vegetable oil
2 tablespoons flour
1 teaspoon prepared hot mustard
1 tablespoon honey
Sea salt and pepper to taste
1 cup milk
1 tablespoon of lemon juice
2 cups crabmeat, cooked
1/4 cup bread crumbs

Preheat oven to 375°. Warm the oil in a skillet over low heat; stir in the flour. Add the mustard, honey, salt and pepper. Gradually pour in the milk and bring the mixture to a simmer, stirring constantly until it thickens. Stir in the lemon juice and crabmeat and remove from stove immediately. Pour into greased, oven-proof cups and sprinkle with the bread crumbs. Bake for 10 minutes or until a light crust forms.

Shrimp Casserole

SERVES 4

2 tablespoons vegetable oil
2 cups shrimp
1 onion, diced
1 green pepper, diced
2 tablespoons wheat flour
1 cup fish stock
2 tablespoons pimento
1/4 teaspoon thyme
1/4 teaspoon paprika
1 bay leaf
1 tablespoon honey

Heat the oil in a skillet; add the shrimp, onion, and pepper and sauté over low heat until golden brown. Add the flour, then gradually pour in the fish stock, stirring constantly until it thickens. Stir in the rest of the ingredients, reduce heat, and simmer for 5 minutes. Serve with brown rice.

Fish and Fowl 89

Honey Flounder

SERVES 4

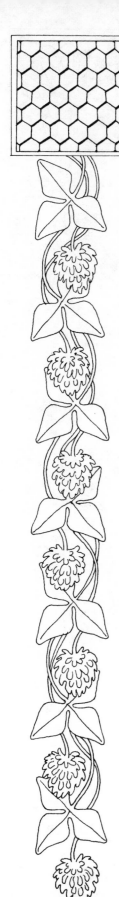

2 cups fish stock
1/2 cup chopped celery
1 small onion, sliced
1 tablespoon fresh lemon juice
1 tablespoon parsley
1 pound flounder fillets
2 tablespoons honey
2 tablespoons flour
1 teaspoon capers

Combine the first 5 ingredients in a saucepan and bring to a boil; reduce heat, add the fillets, and poach at a gentle boil for 15 minutes. Place the fish on a serving dish. Strain the broth from the pan into a bowl and add the honey. Place the flour in another bowl and slowly stir in the strained broth. Pour the broth mixture into a skillet and simmer until it thickens. Pour over the fish, sprinkle with capers, and serve.

Fish Barbecue with Vegetables

SERVES 1

Prepare as many servings in separate foil as needed.

1 small fish, or 1/2 pound frozen fillets
1 large potato, peeled and diced
1 onion, sliced
1/4 cup Parmesan cheese
Sea salt and pepper to taste
4 tablespoons vegetable oil
1/4 cup honey
1 clove garlic, crushed
Juice of one lemon

Spread the diced potato and sliced onion on heavy foil; sprinkle with the cheese, salt, and pepper. Combine 2 tablespoons each of the oil and honey in a bowl; pour over the potato and onion. Fold and seal the edges of the foil and place on a barbecue; grill for 30 minutes, then turn over and cook for 20 minutes more.

Place the fish on another piece of heavy foil; mix the remaining oil and

honey with garlic, salt, and pepper, and spread over the fish; fold and seal the edges of the foil to retain the juices. Place the fish on the barbecue and grill for 20 minutes. Then remove the fish from the barbecue, open the foil, and baste with lemon juice; re-seal, and return to the grill, turning the fish on its opposite side for an additional 20 minutes.

Honey Duck with Prunes

SERVES 4 TO 6

> 1 medium-sized duck
> Sea salt and pepper to taste
> 1/4 cup honey
> 1/2 pound pitted prunes
> 1/4 cup wine (optional)
> 3 tablespoons vinegar
> 1 tablespoon lemon juice
> 1/4 cup honey
> 3 tablespoons port wine, or 1 tablespoon
>   lemon juice and 2 tablespoons water
> 1 tablespoon flour

Preheat oven to 325°. Place the duck in a baking dish and bake for 5 minutes. Remove from oven and season the cavity with salt and pepper; brush the outside of the duck with honey, and prick the skin with a fork. Increase the oven temperature to 350°; return the duck to the oven and roast for 90 minutes.

Combine the prunes, 1/4 cup of wine, vinegar, lemon juice, and honey in a bowl; allow the mixture to stand until the duck is roasted.

When the duck has finished roasting, pour the juice from the baking pan into a skillet; add the prune mixture and bring to a simmer for 10 minutes. To thicken the sauce, gradually add 3 tablespoons of port wine (or 1 tablespoon of lemon juice and 2 tablespoons of water) to 1 tablespoon of flour and add to the sauce. Pour the sauce over the duck, and serve.

Honey Duck

MAKES 4 TO 6 SERVINGS

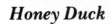
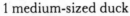

1 medium-sized duck
2 tablespoons sea salt
2 tablespoons honey
2 slices ginger root
2 cloves garlic, crushed
2 scallions chopped
1 1/2 tablespoons natural soy sauce (shoyu)
1 tablespoon orange rind
1/4 teaspoon cinnamon
1/2 cup chicken stock

Basting Sauce:
 3 tablespoons honey
 1 1/2 tablespoons natural soy sauce (shoyu)
 1 tablespoon vinegar
 A dash of sea salt and pepper

Preheat oven to 400°. Pat the duck's cavity dry with a paper towel. Rub the salt on the inside and outside of the duck. Combine the rest of the ingredients in a saucepan over medium heat and bring to a boil; turn off the heat and cool for 3 minutes. Truss the lower cavity of the duck tightly. Stand the duck in a bowl, and pour the hot liquid mixture into the neck opening. Truss the neck.

Fill a roasting pan half full with water; place a rack over the pan. Place the duck on the rack and roast at 400° for 20 minutes, then reduce the heat to 325° and continue roasting for an additional 1 1/2 hours.

Basting Sauce: Combine the basting sauce ingredients in a small bowl; baste the duck with the sauce several times while roasting.

When the duck is roasted, remove from the oven and allow it to stand for 6 to 8 minutes. Remove the trussing from the neck cavity and strain the sauce from the duck into a bowl. Since the duck is hot, handle it very carefully with two forks thrust under the wings, or use clean rubber gloves. Spoon the sauce over the duck and serve.

Honey Orange Duck

MAKES 4 TO 6

1 medium-sized duck
Sea salt and pepper to taste
2 oranges, peeled and sliced into quarters
1 ounce cream cheese
1/2 cup honey
1/2 cup orange juice
1 unpeeled orange, sliced in rounds

Preheat oven to 350°. Rub the cavity of the duck with salt and pepper, and stuff with the quartered oranges and cream cheese; close the opening with skewers. Combine the honey with the orange juice in a bowl and brush the duck several times with the mixture. Roast for 1 hour and 15 minutes, spooning honey and orange sauce over the duck 2 or 3 times while roasting.

When the duck has finished roasting, remove from oven and place on a serving dish. Garnish with the slices of unpeeled orange and serve.

Stuffed Turkey Breast

SERVES 4 TO 5

1 small breast of turkey
1/4 cup water

Dressing:
1/4 cup honey
1 tablespoon lemon juice
2 eggs (optional)
2 tablespoons dry milk
1 cup chopped onions
3 slices San Francisco sourdough bread
2 tablespoons chopped parsley
1/2 teaspoon coarsely ground black pepper
A dash of sea salt
A sprinkling of chives

Preheat oven to 350°. Place the dressing ingredients in a blender and blend at low speed. Stuff the inside of the turkey breast with the dressing, roll up the edges, and close with skewers. Place the turkey in a baking pan with 1/4 cup of water. Bake for 90 minutes or until golden brown.

Fish and Fowl 93

Smoker

Simple Extractor

Straight Knife

Tapered Knife

Spatula

Curved Knife

Wax Knife

Hive with handle for retreiving a Swarm

Lemon Chicken

SERVES 4 TO 5

1 tablespoon vegetable oil
1 medium-sized chicken, cut into serving pieces
1 cup honey
1 tablespoon grated lemon rind
1/4 cup lemon juice
Sea salt and pepper to taste
2 lemons, cut into wedges
1 tablespoon flour
1 cup chicken stock
2 tablespoons chopped parsley
2 tablespoons chopped chives
1 teaspoon marjoram

Preheat oven to 350°. Place the oil in a skillet over medium heat; add the chicken pieces and brown on all sides. Pour the honey into a bowl; dip the chicken pieces into the honey, coating well. Place the chicken in a baking pan and sprinkle with grated lemon rind, lemon juice, salt, and pepper. Arrange the lemon wedges on the chicken, cover the pan with foil, and bake for 45 minutes. Then remove the foil, turn on the broiler, and broil the chicken for 5 minutes. Place the chicken on a serving dish.

Combine the flour with the rest of the ingredients in a saucepan; bring to a boil, reduce heat, and simmer for 5 minutes. Pour the sauce over the chicken and serve immediately. Delicious served with rice or noodles.

Chicken Liver with Grapes or Raisins

SERVES 4

2 cups rice, cooked
2 cups chicken livers, sliced
1/2 cup unbleached white flour
1/2 teaspoon sea salt
1/2 teaspoon pepper
1 cup chicken stock
2 tablespoons sherry (optional)
1 teaspoon thyme
2 tablespoons honey
1 cup grapes or raisins

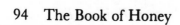

Combine the flour, salt, and pepper in a bowl; dredge the liver pieces in the flour mixture. Coat a skillet with oil and place over medium heat; add the chicken livers and sauté for 2 minutes on each side. Remove the chicken livers from the pan. Combine the chicken stock, sherry, thyme, honey and grapes or raisins in the skillet; reduce heat and simmer until 1/3 of the liquid has evaporated. Place the chicken livers on the rice and cover with the sauce before serving.

Nut Pollo

SERVES 4 TO 5

    2 tablespoons vegetable oil
    1 medium-sized chicken, cut into serving pieces
    1 cup chicken stock
    1 cup walnuts, chopped
    1 onion, chopped
    1 ounce cream cheese
    4 cloves
    4 tablespoons honey
    1/4 teaspoon cinnamon
    1/2 teaspoon chili powder
    2 tablespoons tomato paste
    1/2 cup water
    Sea salt and pepper to taste

Place the oil in a skillet over medium heat; add the chicken pieces and brown on all sides. Pour in the chicken stock, reduce heat, and simmer for 30 minutes, adding water as needed.

Combine the rest of the ingredients in a blender, and blend at medium speed to a coarse purée. Pour the purée into another skillet coated with oil; cook over low heat for 5 minutes, stirring constantly with a wooden spoon. Add the purée to the chicken and continue simmering for 10 to 15 minutes more before serving.

Marinated Chicken

SERVES 4 TO 5

1 medium-sized chicken, cut into serving pieces
1 cup of water
1/2 cup wine vinegar
1/4 cup honey
1 1/2 tablespoons natural soy sauce (shoyu)
Juice of 2 lemons
1 tablespoon orange peel, grated
1/2 teaspoon garlic, crushed
1 teaspoon coarse ground pepper
A sprinkling of ground coriander
A sprinkling of bay leaves
A dash of tabasco

Place the chicken pieces in a deep dish. Combine the rest of the ingredients together in a large bowl, and pour over the chicken. Cover the dish and marinate overnight.

Preheat oven to 450°. Place the marinated chicken pieces in a medium-sized baking pan. Bake for 20–25 minutes; then turn the chicken pieces to brown them evenly, and bake for 40 minutes more.

Isn't it funny
How a bear likes honey?
Buzz! Buzz! Buzz!
I wonder why he does?
—Winnie-the-Pooh, Ch. I

Honey is too good for a bear.
—English proverb

Glazes, Stuffings, Marinades

Honey Pineapple–Mustard Glaze

FOR ONE FOWL

    1/4 cup honey
    1/4 cup pineapple juice (unsweetened)
    1 tablespoon prepared hot mustard
    1 teaspoon natural soy sauce (shoyu)
    1/2 teaspoon white pepper

Combine all the ingredients in a bowl, mixing with a wooden spoon. Cover fowl several times with the glaze before baking; allow a few minutes to elapse between each brushing so the glaze will soak in. *Variation:* Substitute the pineapple juice with 1/4 cup orange juice.

Cooked Marinade

FOR 2 POUNDS POULTRY

    2 cups lightly salted water
    1/2 pound carrots, sliced
    1/2 pound onions, sliced
    10 shallots, chopped
    1 celery stalk, chopped
    2 garlic cloves
    10 peppercorns or 1 teaspoon coarsely ground pepper
    2 cloves
    1/2 cup honey
    1 24-ounce bottle white wine
    1/4 cup vinegar

Combine the ingredients in a large pan and bring to a rolling boil; reduce heat and simmer for 5 minutes. (Do not overboil or the alcohol will evaporate.) Allow the mixture to cool. Pour into a non-metallic container; add poultry and marinate overnight.

Uncooked Marinade

FOR 2 POUNDS POULTRY

1 cup wine vinegar
1 24-ounce bottle white wine (or 12 ounces
  cider vinegar)
1 cup sherry or Madera wine (optional)
4 walnuts
1/2 cup honey
1 teaspoon sage
1 teaspoon sweet basil
1 clove of garlic, whole
1 tablespoon juniper berry
2 cloves
10 whole black peppercorns
1/2 teaspoon coriander
Sea salt to taste

Combine the ingredients in a glass or earthenware bowl, mixing with a wooden spoon. (Do not use metallic containers with marinades.) Add poultry and marinate overnight.

Honey Apple Stuffing

FOR ONE FOWL

2 apples, diced
2 cups raw carrots, grated
2 green peppers, thinly sliced and chopped
1 cup raw summer squash, shredded
2 fresh eggs (optional)
1/2 cup raisins
1 cup mixed nuts, chopped
4 tablespoons honey
1/2 cup bread crumbs
Sea salt and pepper to taste

Combine all the ingredients in a blender at low speed until smooth. Stuff a chicken, duck, or turkey with the mixture. Can also be used to stuff whole tomatoes.

Honey Orange Stuffing

FOR ONE FOWL

1 tablespoon vegetable oil
3 cups bread crumbs
1/4 cup chicken broth
1 cup diced orange
1 tablespoon grated orange rind
1 egg (optional)
1 teaspoon tarragon
1 teaspoon basil
2 tablespoons orange blossom honey
Sea salt and pepper to taste
A dash of Curacao (optional)

Coat a heavy skillet with the oil; place over medium heat; add the bread crumbs and sauté for 2 to 3 minutes, stirring constantly. Gradually pour in the chicken broth, then remove from the heat. Add the rest of the ingredients and toss together. Stuff a duck, cornish hen, or turkey breasts with the mixture.

But Yahweh your God is bringing you into a prosperous land, a land of streams and springs, of waters that well up from the deep in valleys and hills, a land of wheat and barley, of vines, of figs, of pomegranates, a land of olives, of oil, of honey . . .

—Deuteronomy

Vegetarian Casseroles

Spatula

Curved Knife

Wax Knife

Hive with handle for retreiving a Swarm

Vegetarian Casserole

SERVES 4

1 cup cooked brown rice
1 cup ground, roasted peanuts (or pecans,
    walnuts, filberts, Brazil nuts, or a
    combination of these nuts)
1 cup carrots, grated
1/4 cup buckwheat honey
1/2 cup tomatoes, peeled
1 teaspoon natural soy sauce (shoyu)
1 teaspoon chives
Vegetable salt to taste
1 tablespoon vegetable oil
1/2 cup bread crumbs

Preheat oven to 350°. Combine the first 8 ingredients in a large mixing bowl, gently mixing with a wooden spoon. Coat a medium-sized baking pan with the oil and pour in the mixture; sprinkle the top with the bread crumbs. Bake for 45 minutes or until a light crust is formed.

Fresh Almond Casserole

SERVES 2

9 ounces cream cheese or cottage cheese
1 cup chopped almonds
1/2 a sweet red pepper, chopped
1 stalk celery, chopped
1 tablespoon honey
A dash of tabasco
A dash of sea salt
Coarsely ground pepper to taste

Combine the ingredients in a blender at low speed, whipping just long enough to blend the ingredients. Place in a serving dish and chill at least one hour in the refrigerator. Serve with celery and carrot sticks.

102   The Book of Honey

Smoker

Simple Extractor

Straight Knife

Tapered Knife

Honey Bohemienne

SERVES 4

5 large Japanese mushrooms (shiitake), sliced
1 tablespoon corn or sesame oil
1 cup carrots, grated
1 cup celery, chopped
1/2 cup onion, thinly sliced and chopped
1/4 cup unbleached white flour
1/2 envelope dry yeast or 1/2 cake compressed yeast
1 teaspoon sea salt
A dash of white pepper
1 1/2 cups vegetable stock
1 cup cheddar cheese
3/4 cup wheat germ
1/2 cup pecans, chopped
1/2 cup honey
1 tablespoon sesame oil

Spatula

Soak the mushrooms in cold water for about 20 minutes. Coat a large, covered skillet with the oil; place over medium heat and add the mushrooms, carrots, celery, and onion. Reduce heat and simmer until the vegetables are tender, stirring occasionally. Stir in the flour, salt, pepper, and crumble in the yeast. Add the vegetable stock, stirring constantly until the mixture thickens; add the cheese and continue simmering until the cheese melts.

Remove the skillet from the stove; stir in the wheat germ, nuts, and honey. Oil a medium-sized shallow pan, and line the bottom with wax paper. Oil the paper, then pour the mixture into the pan, allowing it to stand for 1 hour.

Preheat oven to 350°. Bake for 45 to 50 minutes, until firm. Remove the pan from the oven and place on a rack for 5 minutes. Serve with Home-made Tomato Paste, or with Honey-Cheese Lasagna Sauce.

Curved Knife

Wax Knife

Hive with handle for retreiving a Swarm

Mushroom Casserole

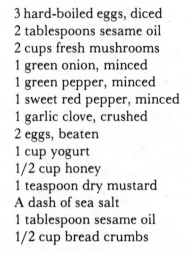

3 hard-boiled eggs, diced
2 tablespoons sesame oil
2 cups fresh mushrooms
1 green onion, minced
1 green pepper, minced
1 sweet red pepper, minced
1 garlic clove, crushed
2 eggs, beaten
1 cup yogurt
1/2 cup honey
1 teaspoon dry mustard
A dash of sea salt
1 tablespoon sesame oil
1/2 cup bread crumbs

Hard boil the eggs in boiling water for 10 minutes; cool by holding them under cold water from the faucet. Shell; then dice the eggs on a plate, and set aside. Place the oil in a large skillet over high heat. Add the mushrooms; sauté 2 minutes over high heat to enhance their flavor, then reduce to low heat. Add the onion, peppers, and garlic to the mushrooms; pour in the eggs, mixing gently with a flat wooden spoon or spatula and simmer for 5 minutes. Blend in the yogurt and honey; add the dry mustard and salt and simmer for 1–2 minutes longer.

Preheat oven to 400°. Coat a baking pan with the oil; pour in the contents of the skillet, and sprinkle the bread crumbs over the top. Cover with foil and bake for 10 minutes. Remove the foil and place under the broiler for 5 minutes or until the top is golden brown.

Cheese Lasagna

SERVES 4

2 tablespoons corn oil
1 medium-sized white or red onion, chopped
2 garlic cloves, minced
1 1/2 pounds peeled tomatoes
1 cup Home-made Tomato Paste
1 teaspoon sea salt
1 teaspoon oregano leaves, crushed
1 teaspoon basil leaves, crushed
A sprinkling of red pepper, crushed
1 tablespoon honey
10 ounces fresh lasagna noodles
1 1/2 cups cottage cheese
1 pound Mozzarella cheese, sliced
1/2 cup Parmesan cheese
1 cup honey roasted peanuts, crushed

Coat a large skillet with the oil and place over medium heat; add the onion and garlic and sauté until the onion turns translucent and the garlic is lightly browned. Add the next 7 ingredients; reduce heat and simmer uncovered for 30 minutes. If the tomato paste is thick, add water to avoid its sticking to the pan.

Fill a large pan with water and salt and bring to a vigorous boil; add the noodles and boil for 10 minutes well covered with water. Drain off the water.

Preheat oven to 375°. Cover the bottom of a medium-sized baking pan (13 x 9 x 2) carefully with 1/3 of the noodles. Dot with 1/3 of the cottage cheese, and cover with 1/3 of the Mozzarella slices, 1/3 cup of the honey roasted nuts, and 1/3 of the sauce. Repeat the process in two more layers. Sprinkle Parmesan cheese on the top and place in the oven for 30 minutes, or until the top becomes crusty. Remove from the oven and allow the lasagna to stand 5 to 7 minutes so the filling will set.

Note: A tablespoon of oil in the cooking water will prevent the noodles from sticking together.

Honey Frijoles

SERVES 4

Legumes in season are a delicacy and should be a part of any vegetable garden. They are high in protein, vitamins, and minerals and low in unsaturated fats. Dry legumes such as kidney, navy, or pinto beans, should be soaked overnight with a dash of baking soda, or boiled for two minutes, allowed to stand for an hour, then cooked slowly over low heat.

> 2 cups kidney beans
> 1 large onion, chopped
> 2 large tomatoes, sliced
> 1 chili pepper, minced
> 2 tablespoons oil (corn or sesame)
> 2 tablespoons honey

Soak the beans in water overnight with a dash of baking soda. Drain off the soaking water, then place the beans in a pan and cover with cold water; bring to a boil, reduce heat and simmer. Add the onion, tomatoes, and chili pepper; cover, and simmer for 2 1/2 hours or until soft. As the liquid in the pan evaporates, add more water so the beans remain covered. When the beans are cooked, drain off the liquid.

Warm the oil and honey in a skillet over low heat; add the beans and simmer for 10 minutes. Then pour the bean mixture into a heat-proof serving dish, and place under a broiler for 7 to 10 minutes until the top turns a light caramel color. Serve hot.

Variation: Pinto beans or lentils can be used in place of kidney beans. Lentils will cook in about 30 minutes and should not soak overnight. If lentils are used, replace the chili pepper with a large celery stalk.

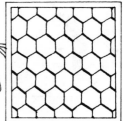

Potato au Gratin

1 teaspoon vegetable oil
4 medium-sized Idaho potatoes, thinly
  sliced in rounds
1/2 cup grated Swiss cheese
1/2 cup grated Parmesan cheese
Sea salt to taste
2 cups yogurt
2 tablespoons honey
1 garlic clove
A sprinkling of nutmeg
1 teaspoon coarse ground black pepper

Preheat oven to 350°. Coat a medium-sized baking pan with oil; arrange a 1–inch layer of potato slices in the bottom of the pan. Sprinkle a portion of the grated cheese and salt over the potatoes; repeat until 3 layers are formed. Combine the rest of the ingredients in a glass or ceramic bowl; pour over the potatoes. Bake for 60 minutes or until a golden crust is formed.

Pumpkin au Gratin

3 pounds pumpkin, peeled and sliced
6 cups water
1/4 teaspoon ground cloves
Sea salt and pepper
1/2 cup heavy cream (or 1/2 cup yogurt)
1/4 cup honey
1 cup Parmesan cheese

Preheat oven to 400°. Place the water and pumpkin in a large pan over high heat and bring to a boil; reduce heat to medium and boil for 15 minutes. Pour off the water.

Mash the pumpkin in the pan with a wooden spoon; stir in the cloves, salt, and pepper. Place the pumpkin in an oiled casserole dish; add the cream and honey, mixing lightly. Sprinkle the top of the mixture with 1 cup of Parmesan cheese. Bake for 30 minutes, or until a light brown crust is formed.

Variation: Squash can be substituted for the pumpkin.

Cumin Rice

SERVES 4

1 cup brown rice, uncooked
2 tablespoons sesame oil (or corn oil)
1/2 cup minced green peppers
1/2 cup onion, sliced thinly and chopped
2 cups chicken stock
2 tablespoons honey
1 tablespoon natural soy sauce (shoyu)
1 teaspoon cumin

Preheat oven to 350°. Place the oil in a skillet over medium heat; add the rice, peppers, and onions, and sauté until golden brown. Turn the rice mixture into a large, oven-proof bowl or pot; add the rest of the ingredients, stir, and cover with a lid or with foil. Bake for 20 to 25 minutes, or until the liquid is absorbed. Fluff with a fork before serving.

Sweet Potato Casserole

SERVES 4

4 medium-sized sweet potatoes, peeled
1/2 cup orange juice
1/2 cup honey
1 tablespoon grated orange rind
1/4 tablespoon ginger
Sea salt to taste
1 teaspoon sesame oil
1 cup cornmeal
1 cup milk or vegetable stock

Preheat oven to 375°. Place the sweet potatoes in a large pan, cover with water and boil until soft. Drain the cooked potatoes well. Combine the sweet potatoes with the next 5 ingredients in a mixing bowl; mash the mixture with a fork until a coarse purée is obtained. Coat a shallow casserole dish with oil and pour in the sweet potato mixture.

Coat a skillet with the oil; add the cornmeal and dry-roast over medium heat, stirring constantly for 5 to 7 minutes. Slowly stir in 1 cup of milk or vegetable stock; bring to a boil over medium high heat, then reduce heat, and simmer for 30 minutes or until the cornmeal thickens. Pour the cornmeal mixture over the sweet potatoes and bake for 30 minutes or until the casserole is bubbling.

Deep South Sweet Potato Pie　　　　SERVES 4

1 1/2 cups yams, cooked and mashed

Crust:
    1 1/2 cups unbleached white flour
    1/2 teaspoon sea salt
    3 tablespoons sesame oil
    1/2 cup water

Filling:
    2 eggs
    6 tablespoons honey
    2/3 cup cream
    1/3 cup orange juice
    A dash of sea salt
    1 teaspoon vanilla
    Freshly ground nutmeg to taste

Cook and mash the yams and set aside in a large bowl.

Crust: Combine the flour and salt in a mixing bowl; add the oil, blending it evenly through the flour by rubbing the mixture between the palms of the hands. Gradually add the water; knead for 10 minutes until smooth. Shape the dough into a ball; wrap in a damp cloth, and place in the refrigerator for 30 minutes.

Filling: Beat the eggs thoroughly in a medium-sized bowl; stir in the rest of the ingredients, mixing well. Pour the mixture into the mashed yams and stir until the combination is a soft purée.

Preheat oven to 450°. Set aside 1/2 cup of dough; roll out the remainder on a floured board to 1/4 inch thickness and place in a 9–inch pie plate. Roll the remaining 1/2 cup of dough into a thin round sheet to fit the top of the pie. Pour the yam filling into the pie plate and place the remaining crust on top. Seal the edges of the pie with the flat side of a fork and prick a few holes in the top to allow moisture to escape.

Bake at 450° for 10 minutes; reduce heat to 350° and bake for 30 minutes longer until the crust is golden brown.

Smoker

Simple Extractor

Straight Knife

Tapered Knife

Spatula

Curved Knife

Wax Knife

Hive with handle for retreiving a Swarm

Cheese Pancake

SERVES 4

    2 medium-sized potatoes, peeled, and sliced
       very thin in rounds
    2 tablespoons vegetable oil
    1/4 cup tofu or sour cream
    2 tablespoons honey
    8 ounces Swiss cheese, or Mozzarella cheese
    Sea salt and pepper to taste

Coat a large frying pan with the oil and place over medium heat; add the potatoes, sautéing until light brown. Reduce heat, cover the pan with a lid, and cook 20 to 30 minutes.

    Combine the tofu (or sour cream) and honey in a bowl, beating with a whisk; pour over the potatoes. Add the cheese, salt, and pepper and stir with a wooden spoon until the cheese threads. Pour the mixture into a baking dish; place under a broiler and broil 8 to 10 minutes, or until the top turns a light brown. Serve piping hot.

Lima Bean Casserole

SERVES 4

    2 cups fresh lima beans
    1 tablespoon vegetable oil
    3 ounces cream cheese or farmer's cheese
    1 small red pepper, thinly sliced
    1 tablespoon honey
    1/2 teaspoon sage
    1 teaspoon parsley
    1 cup bread crumbs
    A dash of sea salt and pepper to taste

Preheat oven to 350°. Shell and cook fresh lima beans in boiling water for 15 minutes with a dash of baking soda. Drain off the water, and place the beans in an oiled, medium-sized baking pan.

    Combine the rest of the ingredients in a blender at low speed for 1 minute; pour over the beans, then cover the pan with foil and bake for 30 minutes. Remove the foil and broil for 5 to 7 minutes or until the top is golden brown. Serve hot with chili sauce or a hotly spiced tomato sauce.

Stuffed Peppers

SERVES 4

2 cups cooked brown rice
1/2 cup soy grits
1 cup tomato paste
1/4 cup celery, chopped
1/4 cup shallots, chopped
1 tablespoon parsley, chopped
Sea salt to taste
1/2 cup honey
4 large green peppers

Preheat oven to 350°. Combine the cooked rice, soy grits, and tomato paste in a large bowl; mix gently with a fork. Add the celery, shallots, parsley, and salt; lightly toss the mixture together. Add the honey in a slow stream, mixing well.

Cut off the top of the peppers (the stem side); scoop out the seeds and stringy pulp. Place the peppers in a pan, cover with water, and bring to a boil over high heat; reduce to medium heat and boil for 5 minutes. Pour off the water. (The peppers should be barely soft.)

Spoon the rice mixture into the pepper shells. Pour 1/2 cup of water into a small and shallow baking pan; stand the stuffed peppers close together in the pan so they remain upright. Bake for 30 minutes. Serve piping hot.

Spatula

Curved Knife

Wax Knife

Hive with handle for retreiving a Swarm

Scrambled Bread Casserole

SERVES 2

1 cup milk
12 ounces stale San Francisco sour dough bread
1/4 cup honey
A sprinkling of cinnamon
Sea salt and pepper to taste
2 tablespoons vegetable oil
6 ounces cheddar cheese, cut in pieces

Pour the milk into a glass bowl; crumble the bread into the milk and allow it to soak. Stir in the honey, cinnamon, salt, and pepper. Coat a skillet with the oil and place over low heat. Pour in the bread and milk; then add the cheese, stirring constantly with a wooden spoon until the cheese threads. Serve immediately.

Vegetarian Casseroles   **111**

Millet Vegetable Scallop

SERVES 4

1 tablespoon sesame oil
2/3 cup millet
2 tablespoons honey
1/3 cup fine bread crumbs
1 cup water
6 cups (1 1/4 lb.) cabbage, coarsely shredded
3 cups carrots, sliced
1 cup onion, thinly sliced
1 1/2 cups chicken stock
1/4 cup milk
1 teaspoon prepared mustard
1 cup Swiss cheese, shredded

Coat a heavy saucepan with oil and place over medium heat; add the millet and sauté, stirring constantly. When the millet begins to brown, add the honey; stir until the honey starts to thicken. Add 1/2 cup of the bread crumbs, stir, remove from the heat, and place immediately in a shallow baking pan.

Bring the cup of water to a boil in a large pan; add the cabbage, carrots, and onion; reduce heat, cover, and simmer for 10 minutes until almost tender. Drain off the water, leaving the vegetables in the pan.

Combine the rest of the ingredients in a bowl; stir into the vegetables, then pour the vegetable mixture into the baking pan. Sprinkle with the remaining crumbs and bake for 30 minutes or until bubbly.

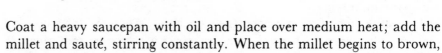

Curried Rice

SERVES 5 TO 6

2 tablespoons vegetable oil
1 thinly sliced onion
2 cups wild rice, cooked
1/2 tablespoon curry
2 tablespoons lemon juice
3 tablespoons honey
1/2 cup pineapple chunks
1 cup grated Cheddar cheese
Sea salt to taste

Place the oil in a large skillet over medium heat; add the onion and saute until brown. Reduce to low heat, add the cooked rice and the rest of the ingredients, stirring constantly until the cheese melts.

The flavor is enhanced if 1/2 cup of Pineapple-Honey Sauce is added and the mixture is allowed to simmer 5 minutes longer.

Honey Stuffed Zucchini

SERVES 8

Stuffed vegetables, with a variety of herbs, are a mainstay in country kitchens all around the Mediterranean. Families pride themselves on their own special recipes. To enhance the taste of the basic recipe below, experiment with a sprinkling of herb(s) such as oregano, basil, bay leaves, thyme, nutmeg, chives, or mother of thyme.

4 medium-sized zucchini
1 cup fresh, cooked kernel corn
1/4 cup milk
1/2 cup creamed cottage cheese or tofu
1/4 cup honey
A dash of sea salt
A dash of pepper
1/2 cup Parmesan cheese
1 tablespoon vegetable oil

Preheat oven to 350°. Wash the zucchini well and cut in half lengthwise; scoop the pulp into a blender. Add the next 6 ingredients; blend at high speed to a purée. Fill the zucchini shells with the mixture; sprinkle with Parmesan cheese. Place the zucchini in a baking pan coated with the oil; bake for 50 minutes, or until zucchini are tender.

Variation: In place of zucchini, use large onions, green peppers, squash, or large, fresh tomatoes. (Choose firm tomatoes, not overly ripe. Place a teaspoonful of uncooked rice in each tomato to absorb the excess liquid—when the tomatoes are cooked so is the rice.)

Grain Fruit Muesli

SERVES 8

3 cups rolled oats
1/2 cup coconut, shredded
1/2 cup raw wheatgerm
1/4 cup sunflower seeds, shelled
1/2 cup almonds, shelled
1/4 cup sesame oil
1/4 cup dark honey
2 tablespoons water
1/2 teaspoon sea salt
1 teaspoon vanilla
1/2 cup raisins
1/2 cup dried apricots, diced
1/2 cup dried figs, diced

Preheat oven to 350° and oil a large baking pan. Combine the first five ingredients in a large bowl. In a smaller bowl, combine the oil, honey, water, salt, and vanilla and add to the dry ingredients, mixing thoroughly. Pour the mixture into the pan; bake for 30 minutes, stirring 2 or 3 times while baking. Remove from oven and cool slightly before adding the raisins and diced fruits. Serve for breakfast.

Fresh Muesli

SERVES 6

1 cup milk
1/2 cup oat flakes
1/4 cup honey
Juice of 1/2 lemon
1/2 cup raisins
2 apples, grated
4 dried figs or dates, sliced
1 banana, sliced
1 tablespoon grated lemon rind
10 walnuts, chopped
10 almonds, chopped

Scald the milk in a medium-sized saucepan. Remove from heat and stir in the oat flakes, honey, lemon juice, and raisins; allow to stand for at least 30 minutes. Combine the fruits and nuts and stir into the mixture. Serve for breakfast with yogurt, kefir, or tofu.

Mighty poor bee that doesn't make more honey than he wants.

—Jamaican proverb

Vegetable and Fruit Side Dishes

Honey Carrots and Peas

SERVES 6

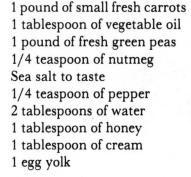

1 pound of small fresh carrots
1 tablespoon of vegetable oil
1 pound of fresh green peas
1/4 teaspoon of nutmeg
Sea salt to taste
1/4 teaspoon of pepper
2 tablespoons of water
1 tablespoon of honey
1 tablespoon of cream
1 egg yolk

Blanch the carrots in a saucepan with water to cover. Drain off the water and place the carrots in a pan coated with the oil. Add the peas, nutmeg, salt, and pepper. Cover, and cook over low heat for five minutes. Shake the saucepan to prevent sticking or excessive browning. Stir in the water and the honey; simmer 10 minutes or until tender.

Remove from heat and pour the vegetables into a serving bowl. Combine the cream with the egg yolk in a small bowl and pour over the vegetables, mixing gently.

Honey Sweet Potatoes

SERVES 4 TO 6

4 sweet potatoes, peeled
1/4 cup honey
1 cup fresh orange juice
Sea salt to taste
A dash of tabasco

Preheat oven to 350°. Slice the potatoes lengthwise, then cut in quarters; place in a pan with water to cover and boil for 15 minutes. Pour off the water. Coat a medium-sized baking pan with oil; place the potato pieces in the pan and add honey, orange juice, salt, and tabasco. Bake for 35 minutes, or until a light brown crust is formed on the potatoes.

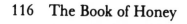

Glazed Carrots SERVES 4

    2 cups water
    1 pound carrots, sliced in small strips
    1 tablespoon honey
    1 tablespoon olive oil
    A dash of sea salt
    1 tablespoon parsley

Place the water in a covered skillet and bring to a boil; add the carrots, reduce heat and boil gently for 20 minutes. Drain the water from the carrots. Combine the carrots, honey, olive oil, and the salt in a saucepan over medium heat; cook uncovered for 5 to 7 minutes, gently stirring the carrots until they are glazed. Pour into a serving dish, and sprinkle with parsley.

Honey Fresh Green Peas SERVES 4

    2 cups of fresh green peas, shelled
    A dash of sea salt
    1 teaspoon of honey

Bring water to a boil in a saucepan. Add the green peas and salt; reduce heat and simmer for 15 minutes. Drain off the water and pour the peas into a serving dish; add the honey, mixing lightly. Serve with poultry.

Smoker

Simple Extractor

Straight Knife

Tapered Knife

Spatula

Curved Knife

Wax Knife

Hive with handle for retreiving a Swarm

Honeyed Yams and Apples

SERVES 6

4 sweet potatoes, peeled
2 large, tart apples, peeled and cored
1 cup honey
1 cup chopped walnuts
Sea salt and pepper to taste
1/4 cup vegetable oil
1/2 cup almonds, slivered

Preheat oven to 350°. Slice the potatoes and the apples into rounds. Coat a 10" x 14" baking pan with oil; arrange a layer of potatoes and apples in the bottom of the pan. Cover with a portion of the honey, walnuts, salt, and pepper. Repeat the process with each layer.

Pour the oil into a skillet over medium heat; sauté the almonds for 5 minutes, stirring constantly. Sprinkle the almonds over the top layer of potatoes and apples. Bake for 30 minutes, or until the top turns a light brown.

Braised Lettuce

SERVES 2 TO 3

1 tablespoon vegetable oil
2 pounds lettuce, shredded
2 small onions, diced
1 tablespoon honey
1/2 teaspoon thyme
1/2 teaspoon sweet basil
Sea salt and pepper to taste

Combine all of the ingredients together in a skillet over low heat; cover, and simmer for 45 minutes. Add water only if necessary to avoid browning the mixture too rapidly.

Honey Bananas

SERVES 3 TO 4

2 large bananas, cut into finger-sized slices
Corn oil for deep frying
1/2 cup honey
1/4 cup sesame seeds

Combine the honey and sesame seeds in a bowl. Fill a heavy skillet or deep fryer with 3 inches of oil and heat to 350°. Dip each banana finger in the bowl of honey and seeds, coating thoroughly. Drop immediately into the hot oil for 3 to 5 minutes, or until crisp, golden, and caramelized. Drain on absorbent paper before serving.

Variation: (1) Deep fry finger-sized slices of banana until crisp; drain on absorbent paper, and place in a shallow dish. Combine 2 tablespoons vinegar, 1/2 cup honey, and 1/4 cup water in a saucepan; simmer until the mixture thickens, stirring constantly. Pour the syrup over the bananas and sprinkle with sesame seeds. Set the syrup by placing the dish on a bed of crushed ice for 30 minutes.

(2) Slice the bananas in half lengthwise. Place in a baking dish with a tablespoon of water. Combine 1/4 cup of honey, 1 tablespoon of rum, 1 tablespoon of lime juice, and a dash of salt in a bowl. Pour over the bananas. Broil for 7 to 10 minutes, or until the syrup thickens.

(3) Sliced apples, grapefruit, pineapple, and yams—or cherries and grapes—can be used in place of bananas.

Honeyed Pineapple

SERVES 4

1 fresh pineapple
1 tablespoon water
1/2 cup honey
1 tablespoon lemon juice
A dash of sherry (optional)
Sea salt and pepper to taste

Preheat oven to 350°. Peel the pineapple and cut it into 4 thick slices; place in a medium-sized baking pan with one tablespoon water. Combine the honey, lemon juice, salt, and pepper in a bowl, mixing thoroughly; pour over the pineapple. Bake for 20 minutes. Serve in 4 individual bowls; add a dash of sherry if desired.

Vegetable and Fruit Side Dishes 119

Natural Potato Chips

SERVES 2

1 medium–sized potato, unpeeled

Wash the potato carefully, and slice into thin rounds. Place the rounds on a greased cookie sheet, three inches from the broiler, for 10 minutes, or until the side under the broiler puffs up and browns slightly. Take the cookie sheet out of the oven and with a flat wooden spatula (or spoon), carefully turn over each piece. Return to the broiler for 5 to 6 minutes, or until puffed and brown. Remove and serve immediately with any honey spread or dip.

Honeyed Apples

SERVES 4

1/4 cup honey
A dash of cognac (optional)
1 teaspoon grated orange peel
Sea salt and white pepper to taste
4 large, tart apples
1 tablespoon water

Preheat oven to 350°. Combine the first 4 ingredients in a small bowl. Core the apples and place in a baking pan with a tablespoon of water. Pour the honey mixture into the apples, filling the inside of each. Bake for 35 minutes. Serve warm, or allow to cool before serving.

Honeyed Grapefruit

SERVES 4

2 grapefruit
1/4 cup honey
A dash of Angostura bitters
Sea salt and white pepper to taste

Slice the grapefruit in halves and place in a baking pan. Combine the rest of the ingredients in a bowl and pour over the top of the grapefruit. Place under a broiler for 10 minutes.

Thy lips, O my spouse, drop as the honey-comb: honey and milk are under thy tongue; and the smell of thy garments is like the smell of Lebanon.

—The Song of Songs (IV)

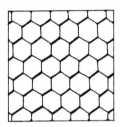

Desserts

Honey Vanilla Ice Cream SERVES 8

Ice Cream sweetened with honey is not as firm as regular ice cream, but the flavor is much better.

    2 vanilla beans, chopped
    1/2 cup water
    2 eggs
    1/2 cup honey
    2 cups milk
    2 tablespoons arrowroot
    1 tablespoon gelatin unflavored, or 1 stick agar
    2 cups heavy cream, whipped

Bring the water to a boil in a saucepan; add the vanilla beans, cover, and boil for 1 minute. Allow the mixture to stand overnight.

Pour the beans and water into a blender and purée until smooth; strain through a mesh strainer, reserving the liquid. Combine the eggs, honey, milk, arrowroot, and gelatin (or agar) in a saucepan and slowly bring to a boil; reduce and simmer until the mixture thickens, stirring constantly. Pour into a bowl and place in the refrigerator for 30 minutes.

Remove the egg mixture from the refrigerator and stir in the vanilla bean liquid; then fold in the whipped cream. Pour the mixture into 2 freezer trays; place in the freezer for 5 to 10 minutes, or until the mixture freezes around the edges of each pan while the centers remain soft. Remove from freezer and pour into a blender, mixing at low speed until a smooth paste forms. Pour the mixture back into the trays and return to the freezer for 30 minutes or until firm.

Variation: Add one chopped banana or 1/2 cup berries to the mixture before placing in the blender.

Easy Honey Ice Cream

SERVES 6

2 cups heavy cream, whipped
2 eggs, separated
1/2 cup honey
1 teaspoon vanilla

Beat the egg yolks in a medium-sized bowl until thick, gradually adding the honey until it is thoroughly combined. Add the vanilla, and fold in the whipped cream. Place the bowl in the freezer for 5 to 6 minutes until the mixture freezes around the edges; the center should remain soft. Remove from the freezer and add the egg whites, beating until smooth. Pour into a freezer tray and return to the freezer until the ice cream is firm and ready to serve.

Honey Meringue

MAKES 8 TO 10

Meringues are a traditional Mediterranean treat; they are displayed in fluffy mounds in the windows of European "pâtisseries" or pastry shops.

4 egg whites
A dash of sea salt
1 cup honey
1 tablespoon unbleached white flour

Preheat oven to 275°. Fill a large bowl with cold water; drain, but do not wipe dry. (This prevents the meringue from sticking to the bowl.) Place the egg whites in the bowl; add the salt, and beat until they form stiff, but not dry, peaks. Pour the honey in a fine stream over the egg whites, beating constantly for about 10 to 15 minutes until the meringue retains its shape. Add the flour to the mixture, blending well.

Oil a cookie sheet and lightly dust it with flour; scoop the meringue mixture onto the sheet with a tablespoon in small mounds. Place in the oven and bake for 30 minutes or until a thin, hard crust forms; do not brown.

Variation: Sprinkle pine nuts over the meringues before placing them in the oven.

Mousse Freeze

SERVES 6

3 eggs
3/4 cup honey
1 cup heavy cream
1/4 cup pistachio nuts, chopped

Separate 2 of the eggs, putting the yolks in 1 bowl and the whites into another. Beat the 2 egg yolks with the remaining whole egg until light. Add the honey to the eggs in a slow stream beating constantly until thoroughly blended. Place the egg yolk mixture in a double boiler over low heat and cook until thickened. Pour into a large bowl, allow to cool, then place in the refrigerator for 30 minutes.

Beat the egg whites in a bowl until stiff. Whip the cream in a separate bowl. Gently fold the egg white into the chilled egg yolk mixture until no large areas of white remain; fold in the cream.

Spoon into individual serving dishes. Sprinkle with the nuts and place in the refrigerator overnight before serving.

Variation: For a chocolate flavor, mix 1 tablespoon carob powder into the yolk mixture after the honey has been added.

Baked Custard

MAKES 6 CUPS

3 eggs
1/2 cup honey
1/2 teaspoon sea salt
3 cups milk
1/2 teaspoon vanilla
1/4 teaspoon nutmeg

Preheat oven to 350°. Blend the first 3 ingredients together in a bowl; add the milk, stirring constantly; then add the vanilla. Pour the mixture into custard cups and sprinkle with nutmeg. Cover the bottom of a shallow baking pan with 1/2 inch of water; place the 6 custard cups in the pan and bake for 30 to 35 minutes. Serve warm, or chill in the refrigerator before serving.

Raisin Bread Pudding

SERVES 6 TO 8

3/4 cup honey
4 cups whole wheat bread cubes
1 quart milk
5 eggs
3/4 cup raisins
1/4 teaspoon nutmeg

Preheat oven to 350°. Combine 1/2 cup of the honey and the bread cubes in a large pan. Place over low heat until the honey is absorbed by the bread (about 3 minutes). Combine the milk, eggs, and the remaining 1/4 cup of honey in a blender at medium speed and add to the bread cubes; stir in the raisins.

Pour into a greased, medium-sized baking pan and sprinkle with nutmeg. Place the baking pan inside a larger pan containing 1 inch of water. Bake for 60 minutes, or until a knife inserted into the center of the pudding comes out clean. Serve topped with Honey Yogurt Sauce.

Variation: Substitute the raisins with 1 cup of fresh seedless grapes or pitted bing cherries.

Rice Pudding

SERVES 4

1 1/2 cups white or brown rice, cooked
2 cups milk (soy or dairy)
1/2 cup dark honey
1 vanilla bean, or 1 teaspoon powdered vanilla
1 cup dried apricots, diced
1 teaspoon cinnamon

Preheat oven to 350°. Combine all of the ingredients in a mixing bowl, blending thoroughly. Pour the mixture into a 1-quart baking pan; dust with cinnamon and bake for 90 minutes. The pudding is ready when a knife inserted into its center comes out clean. Serve either warm or chilled with a honey sauce.

Variation: Substitute the apricots with dried fruits such as pitted prunes, apples, peaches, dates, or raisins.

Spatula

Curved Knife

Wax Knife

Hive with handle for retrieving a Swarm

Doughnuts

MAKES 16

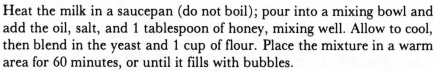

2/3 cup milk
2 tablespoons vegetable oil
1/4 teaspoon sea salt
1/3 cup honey
1/2 cake yeast, crumbled
3 cups unbleached white flour, sifted
1 egg, beaten
3/4 teaspoon cinnamon
1/4 teaspoon nutmeg
Oil for deep frying

Heat the milk in a saucepan (do not boil); pour into a mixing bowl and add the oil, salt, and 1 tablespoon of honey, mixing well. Allow to cool, then blend in the yeast and 1 cup of flour. Place the mixture in a warm area for 60 minutes, or until it fills with bubbles.

Combine the egg, spices, and the rest of the honey and stir into the bubbling mixture; add the remaining flour and mix until a dough forms. Turn the dough onto a floured board and knead for 1 minute; then place the dough in a bowl, cover with a cloth, and allow it to rise until double in size (about 1 1/2 hours). Punch down and place the dough on the floured board; roll until 1/2 inch thick. Cut the dough with a floured doughnut-cutter, cover with a damp cloth, and allow the doughnuts to rise for 1 1/2 hours.

Bring the oil to frying temperature in a skillet, or deep-fryer (360°); drop the doughnuts into the oil and fry for 1 minute on each side. Remove and drain on absorbent paper.

Variation: For a delicious glaze, dip the fried doughnuts into honey warmed in a double boiler. Place on a rack to dry.

Honey Crêpes

1 1/4 cups milk
1 egg
1 egg yolk
1 tablespoon sesame or corn oil
1 cup whole wheat or rice flour
A dash of sea salt
1 cup honey
1 cup chopped almonds (or other nuts)

Blend the first 6 ingredients together in a mixing bowl until smooth. Allow the mixture to stand for one hour.

Lightly coat the bottom of an omelette pan or small frying pan with a small amount of oil and place over medium heat. Pour 2 tablespoons of batter into the pan; cook for one minute, turn, and cook 1 minute more. Lightly oil the bottom of the pan between each crêpe.

Spread a teaspoonful each of the honey and almonds on the individual crêpes and gently fold or roll.

Banana Fritters

MAKES 6 SERVINGS

6 bananas, sliced lengthwise
1/2 cup rum (optional)
1/2 cup honey
1 teaspoon cinnamon
1 cup unbleached white flour
1 cup milk
1 tablespoon oil
A dash of sea salt
Oil for deep frying (at least 3 cups)

Place the sliced bananas lengthwise in a shallow pan. Combine the rum, honey, and cinnamon and pour over the bananas; allow the bananas to stand for 30 minutes.

Combine the next 4 ingredients and blend to form a batter. Heat the oil to 375° in a skillet or deep-fryer; dip the banana slices in the batter and deep fry for 3 to 5 minutes until golden brown. Drain on paper towels and serve hot.

Variation: Bananas Flambé: Pour 3 ounces of rum over the bananas and light with a long match.

Curled Honey and Cinnamon Wafers

MAKES 1 DOZEN

1/4 cup oil
1 cup honey
1/2 cup unbleached white flour, sifted
1/2 teaspoon cinnamon
1/2 teaspoon grated orange rind
1/4 cup slivered almonds
1 egg

Combine the oil and honey in a small bowl. Sift the flour and cinnamon together into a mixing bowl; add the orange rind, nuts, and the egg, beating well. Stir in the oil and honey mixture, and allow the batter to stand for 30 minutes.

Preheat oven to 300°. Drop 1/4 teaspoonful of batter for each cookie onto a heavily greased pan and flatten with a knife; allow 1 inch space between each cookie. Bake for 10 minutes; remove from the oven and cool for 1 minute. Lift the cookies from the pan and roll into cone shapes. Return the cookies to the pan and bake 6 to 10 minutes until golden brown. Serve with honey.

Chowmein Noodle Cookies

MAKES 3 DOZEN

1 cup honey
1 cup nut butter
1/4 cup milk
1 teaspoon vanilla
2 tablespoons unbleached white flour
3 ounce can chowmein noodles

Combine the honey, nut butter, milk, vanilla and flour in a mixing bowl; fold in the noodles. Blend with a wooden spoon, then knead for 8 to 10 minutes, or until a dough forms. Wrap a damp cloth around the dough and chill in the refrigerator for 30 minutes.

Preheat oven to 325°. Drop teaspoonfuls of the dough onto a greased cookie sheet; leave 1-inch space between each cookie. Bake for 20 minutes, or until golden brown. Cool on racks.

Honey Cookies

MAKES 3 DOZEN

1/2 cup vegetable oil
1/2 cup honey
1 3/4 cups unbleached white flour
1 teaspoon baking soda
1/2 teaspoon cinnamon
1/4 teaspoon ground cloves
1/3 cup wheat germ

Combine oil and honey in a mixing bowl. Sift the flour, soda, cinnamon, and cloves together into a separate bowl and gradually add to the honey mixture; stir in the wheat germ. Allow to stand overnight, or chill in the refrigerator for one hour.

Preheat oven to 350°. Place the dough on a lightly floured board and roll to 1/8-inch thickness. Cut the dough into desired shapes with floured cutters and place on a greased cookie sheet. Bake for 10 minutes. Delicious plain or coated with a honey frosting.

Carob (Chocolate) Oatmeal Cookies

MAKES 6 DOZEN

2 1/2 cups unbleached white flour, sifted
1 teaspoon baking soda
1 teaspoon cinnamon
1/2 teaspoon sea salt
A dash of pepper
1 cup oil
1 1/4 cups honey
1 1/2 cups rolled oats
2 eggs, beaten
4 tablespoons carob powder
1 cup nuts, chopped

Sift the first 5 ingredients together into a mixing bowl. Combine the oil and honey in a separate bowl, and add to the flour mixture. Add the remaining ingredients and mix well in the bowl, or transfer to a blender and mix at low speed. Allow the batter to stand for 30 minutes.

Preheat oven to 325°. Drop a teaspoonful of batter for each cookie onto a greased cookie sheet; leave 1-inch space between each cookie. Bake for 20 minutes, or until golden brown.

Desserts 129

Carob (Chocolate) Cake

    2 1/2 cups unbleached white flour
    1/2 teaspoon baking soda
    1 teaspoon baking powder
    1/2 teaspoon sea salt
    1/4 cup water
    1/2 cup buttermilk
    1 cup honey
    1/2 cup vegetable oil
    1 teaspoon vanilla
    1 egg, separated
    1/2 cup carob powder

Preheat oven to 350°. Oil a medium-sized baking pan. Sift together the flour, baking soda, baking powder, and salt into a mixing bowl. Graudally add the water and buttermilk, mixing well. Combine the honey and oil in another bowl and add to the flour mixture. Beat the vanilla, egg yolk, and carob in a small bowl; stir into the mixture, blending until smooth. Beat the egg white stiff and fold into the batter. Pour the batter into the pan and bake for 50 minutes, or until a knife inserted into the center of the cake comes out clean. Serve plain or with frosting.

Cheese Cake

Crust:
- 1 cup granola
- 1 tablespoon honey
- 1 tablespoon lemon juice

Filling:
- 3 tablespoons sesame butter
- 2 cups cottage cheese, well drained
- 2 tablespoons wholegrain flour
- 1/2 teaspoon sea salt
- 1/4 cup fresh lemon juice
- 1 tablespoon grated lemon rind
- 1 cup honey

Preheat oven to 350°. *Crust:* Combine the granola, honey, and lemon juice in a bowl; mix well. Spoon the mixture into a 9-inch pie plate and press with a spoon or fingers to form an even crust inside the pan.

Filling: Combine the butter, cottage cheese, flour, and salt in a mixing bowl or blender at low speed. Add the remaining ingredients and blend until smooth. Pour the filling into the pie shell and bake for 60 minutes. Chill for easy slicing. Serve with honey strawberry jam.

Variation: Substitute the granola in the crust with 2 cups of Graham cracker crumbs. For a lighter filling, beat 2 egg whites and fold into the filling mixture.

Honey Yogurt Apple Cake

1 cup honey
1 cup sesame oil
2 eggs, beaten lightly
1 teaspoon vanilla
2 cups unbleached white flour
1 teaspoon baking powder
1 teaspoon baking soda
A dash of sea salt
1 cup plain natural yogurt
2 cups apples, peeled and diced

Preheat oven to 350°. Grease three 8 x 5 x 1-inch pans.

Combine the honey, oil, eggs, and vanilla in a large bowl, mixing well. Sift together the flour, baking powder, baking soda, and salt into another bowl. Gradually add the yogurt, alternating with the flour, to the honey and egg mixture; beat until smooth. Fold in the apples.

Pour one third of the batter into each pan; cover the batter with your favorite topping and bake for 45 minutes. Layer, and serve as 1 cake or use as 3 separate cakes.

Carrot-Almond Cake

5 medium-sized carrots, peeled and grated
1/2 cup almonds, sliced
1 teaspoon baking soda
1 teaspoon cinnamon
1 1/2 cups whole wheat flour
2 tablespoons cooking oil
2 tablespoons buttermilk
1/2 cup honey
1 egg

Combine the carrots, almonds, baking soda, cinnamon, and flour in a mixing bowl. Beat the oil, buttermilk, honey, and egg together in another bowl and add to the carrot mixture. Pour the batter into the top half of a double boiler that has been greased and floured; cover and steam for 3 hours. Do not allow the boiler to run dry; add boiling water if necessary.

When the cake has finished cooking, allow it to cool for 10 minutes, then turn onto a cake plate and serve plain or with frosting or topping.

Haman's Pockets:
Honey Pastry Squares

MAKES 4 DOZEN

    4 cups unbleached white flour
    2 teaspoons baking powder
    1/2 teaspoon sea salt
    3/4 cup vegetable oil
    3/4 cup honey
    4 eggs
    1/4 cup orange juice
    Poppy Seed or Prune Filling

Sift the first three ingredients together in a bowl and form a well in the center of the mixture. Combine the oil, honey, eggs, and orange juice in a separate bowl; pour into the well and mix thoroughly with a wooden spoon until a dough forms. Knead the dough for 10 minutes or until smooth. Chill in the refrigerator for 2 hours.

    Preheat oven to 350°. Remove the dough from the refrigerator and place on a floured board; roll until 1/4 inch thick. Cut the dough into 4-inch squares and place a tablespoon of Poppy Seed or Prune Filling in center of square. Fold over to form a triangle, and seal the edges with a fork. Place on a greased cookie sheet and bake for 20 minutes or until light brown.

Haman's Pockets:
Poppy Seed Filling

FILLING FOR 4 DOZEN

    3 cups boiling water
    2 cups poppy seeds
    1 cup honey
    1 cup milk
    2 tablespoons grated lemon rind

Steep the poppy seeds in the boiling water for 10 minutes. Pour off the water and place the seeds in a blender at low speed until well ground. Combine the seeds with the honey, milk, and lemon rind in a saucepan; place over low heat, stirring until thick. Remove from heat and allow the mixture to cool. Use as a filling for pastry squares.

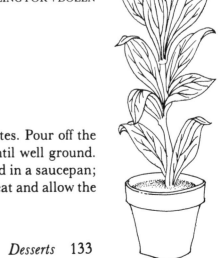

Smoker

Simple Extractor

Straight Knife

Tapered Knife

Spatula

Curved Knife

Wax Knife

Hive with handle for retreiving a Swarm

Haman's Pockets:
Prune Filling

FILLING FOR 4 DOZEN

    1 pound pitted prunes, uncooked
    1 cup honey
    4 tablespoons lemon juice
    2 tablespoons grated lemon rind

Combine all the ingredients in a blender at low speed, blending until smooth. Use as a filling for pastry squares.

Honey Cake for Rosh Hashanah

SERVES 8

    4 eggs
    2 cups honey
    1/2 cup strong coffee
    2 tablespoons vegetable oil
    3 1/2 cups unbleached white flour
    1 1/2 tablespoons baking powder
    1 teaspoon baking soda
    1 teaspoon cinnamon
    1 teaspoon allspice
    1/4 teaspoon sea salt
    3/4 cup candied fruit
    3/4 cup blanched almonds
    1/4 cup brandy

Preheat oven to 325°. Grease and flour a large 9-inch loaf pan.

Place the eggs in a mixing bowl and beat with a whisk; then add the honey, coffee, and oil, mixing well. Sift together the flour, baking powder, baking soda, spices, and salt into a separate bowl; add the fruits and nuts. Combine all the ingredients together in the mixing bowl or transfer to a blender, mixing until creamy smooth. Add the brandy when the batter is creamy. Pour the cake mixture into the pan and bake for 50 to 60 minutes.

Honey Halva *(A Traditional Jewish Recipe)* SERVES 8

1 cup honey
3/4 cup nut butter, preferably tahini
4 eggs
2 cups semolina
1 cup almonds, chopped
1 teaspoon powdered cinnamon

Syrup:
3 cups water
2 cups honey

Preheat oven to 350°. Oil a 3-inch-deep baking pan. Combine the first two ingredients in a mixing bowl and add the eggs one by one, beating constantly. Stir in the semolina, almonds, and cinnamon. Pour the batter into the pan, and bake for 35 to 40 minutes. Remove from oven and place the baked halva on a serving dish.

Syrup: Combine the water and honey in a saucepan and bring to a boil; reduce heat and simmer until the syrup thickens, stirring constantly. Pour the warm syrup over the halva.

Honey Pie Crust *(Basic Recipe)* 1 9-INCH PIE CRUST

1 1/4 cups whole wheat flour
1 tablespoon honey
7 tablespoons sesame oil
1 tablespoon cold water

Combine all the ingredients in a bowl, blending thoroughly. Press the dough firmly onto the bottom and sides of a 9-inch pie pan. This pie crust can be used with any filling.

Desserts 135

Honey Pie Filling

FILLING FOR 1 PIE

1 Honey Pie Crust

1/4 cup honey
2 egg yolks
3 tablespoons flour
A dash of sea salt
2 cups milk

Preheat oven to 350°. Combine the first four ingredients together in a saucepan, blending thoroughly. Stir in the milk and place over low heat, stirring constantly for 5 minutes or until thick. Pour the filling into a 9-inch pie shell and bake for 60 minutes.

Carob Filling

MAKES 1 1/2 CUPS

1/3 cup nut butter
1/3 cup carob powder
3 tablespoons milk
2 tablespoons honey
1 cup powdered milk

Combine all the ingredients in a mixing bowl and beat until smooth. Use as a filling in layer cakes.

Pecan Pie Filling

FILLING FOR 1 PIE

1 Honey Pie Crust

1 cup honey
1/2 cup sesame butter
3 eggs, beaten
1/4 cup nonfat dry milk
1 1/2 cups pecans, chopped
1 teaspoon cinnamon
1 teaspoon vanilla

Preheat oven to 350°. Combine the honey and sesame butter together in a bowl. Add the beaten eggs and dry milk, mixing well; if too thick, add a little water. Stir in the remaining ingredients. Pour the filling into a pie shell and bake for 60 minutes.

136   The Book of Honey

Easter Pie (Melopitta)

MAKES 1 PIE

Melopitta is a traditional dish served in Greek homes at Easter as well as at other times of the year.

1 Honey Pie Crust

1 pound cottage cheese
1 cup honey
4 eggs
1 tablespoon cinnamon, powdered

Preheat oven to 350°. Combine the cottage cheese and honey together in a bowl. Beat the eggs well, then add to the cheese and honey mixture, mixing thoroughly. Pour the filling into the pie crust and bake for 30 minutes. Remove the pie from the oven and sprinkle with cinnamon. Cool before serving.

Pumpkin Pie

FILLING FOR 1 PIE

1 Honey Pie Crust

6 tablespoons honey
1 cup light cream
2 cups unsweetened pumpkin purée
1 teaspoon cinnamon
1/2 teaspoon ginger
1/2 teaspoon mace
1/2 teaspoon ground cloves
A dash of sea salt
1 egg, beaten (optional)

Preheat oven to 450°. Pour the honey into a mixing bowl and slowly stir in the cream. Add the pumpkin purée, mixing well. Add the rest of the ingredients and mix until thoroughly blended. Pour the filling into a pie shell and bake for 10 minutes. Reduce the oven temperature to 325° and bake for 40 to 45 minutes longer or until the filling is set.

Lick honey with your little finger.
—English proverb

Spreads, Toppings, Dips, and Snacks

Peanut, sesame seek, almond, and cashew butters are excellent sources of minerals and proteins and constitute a high protein snack when combined with honey on whole grain bread.

Honey butters, syrups, spreads, purées, toppings, and frostings can be served over puddings, cakes, toasts, and muffins. They enhance the flavor of baked goods and, in addition, they provide energy and wholesomeness.

Nut Butters: Combine the nuts and oil in a blender at medium speed. Blend until the nut butter reaches the desired consistency.

Peanut Butter

> 1 cup roasted or raw peanuts
> 4 tablespoons peanut oil

Sesame Butter

> 1 cup roasted sesame seeds
> 4 tablespoons sesame oil

Tahini

> 1 cup raw sesame seeds
> 4 tablespoons sesame oil

Almond Butter

> 1 cup almonds
> 4 tablespoons vegetable oil

Cashew Butter

> 1 cup cashews
> 4 tablespoons peanut oil

Honey Butter

> 1 cup of any nut butter
> 1 cup honey

Allow the butter to soften at room temperature. Add the honey and beat until smooth and creamy.

Fluffy Frosting

MAKES 1 CUP

> 2 egg whites
> A dash of sea salt
> 1/2 cup honey

Combine the egg whites with salt in a bowl; beat until stiff peaks are formed. Pour the honey in a fine stream over the egg white, beating constantly for 2 minutes (4 minutes by hand) until smooth and creamy. *Variation:* Add 1/2 teaspoon of grated orange rind to the egg whites along with the honey. Spread over any one-layer cake or angel cake.

Fruit Topping

MAKES 1 CUP

> 1/4 cup nut butter
> 1/2 cup honey
> 4 tablespoons of orange juice (or any fresh
>   fruit juice)

Soften the butter in a saucepan over very low heat. Add the remaining ingredients and stir for 2 minutes. Pour into a blender at low speed and mix to a creamy paste.

Cranberry Topping

MAKES 1 CUP

> 1 cup cranberries, minced
> 1/4 cup honey

Combine ingredients in a bowl, mixing well. Pour over a cheese cake, or any soft cake, before baking.
Variation: Substitute any berries in season for the cranberries.

Crumb Topping

MAKES 1 1/2 CUPS

    4 tablespoons honey
    4 tablespoons nut butter
    1/4 cup unbleached white flour
    1/4 cup bread crumbs
    1/2 teaspoon grated lemon peel
    1/4 to 1/2 cup water

Combine the honey and butter together in a bowl; add the remaining ingredients and mix thoroughly. Coat a cheese cake with this topping before baking.

Honey Orange Syrup

MAKES 1 CUP

    2/3 cup honey
    1/3 cup fresh orange juice

Combine the honey and orange juice in a blender at high speed. Chill. Serve over muffins, toast, and pancakes.
Variation: Substitute the orange juice with fruit juices such as apricot, peach, grapefruit, grape, or pineapple.

English Rose Honey

MAKES 1/2 CUP

    1/2 cup mild honey
    1/2 cup rose petals

Place the petals in a wooden bowl and mash thoroughly with a pestle. Combine the crushed rose petals and honey in a saucepan and warm over low heat for no more than 3 minutes. Strain the mixture through a fine mesh strainer and pour into a glass, ceramic, or earthenware jar; seal tightly. Allow the jar to stand in a warm room for one week.
    For a stronger fragrance, do not strain the honey.

Wilderness Honey

MAKES 1/2 GALLON

18 fireweed blossoms
30 red clover blossoms
30 white clover blossoms
2 cups water
10 cups clover honey
1 teaspoon alum

Combine the blossoms and water in a large pan and boil for 5 minutes until blossoms are soft. Allow the mixture to stand overnight. Return the pan to the stove and bring to a boil once again; add the honey and alum and simmer for 10 minutes. Strain the mixture through a fine mesh strainer; pour into sterilized jars, and seal.

Honey Almond Spread

MAKES 1 1/2 CUPS

1 cup shelled almonds
1 teaspoon sesame oil
1/2 cup honey

Combine the almonds and oil in a blender at medium speed until the almonds have a paste-like consistency; add the honey and blend well. Spread on toast and muffins; or serve with curled honey and cinnamon wafers.

Honey Spread à la Maître d'H.

MAKES 2/3 CUP

1/4 pound butter
1/4 cup honey
1/2 cup lemon juice
Sea salt and pepper to taste
1 tablespoon parsley

Melt the butter in a skillet over low heat; add the next 3 ingredients and simmer for 3 minutes, stirring with a wooden spoon. Pour into a serving bowl and sprinkle parsley over the top. Serve warm on toast.

Honey Strawberry Butter

MAKES 2 CUPS

1/4 cup nut butter
1/2 cup honey
1 1/2 cups fresh strawberries

Place the ingredients in a blender and whirl at high speed until smooth.
Variation: In place of the strawberries, substitute 1 1/2 cups blueberries,
raspberries, or gooseberries. Add a teaspoon of lemon rind to enhance
the flavor of the berries.

Rose Hip Butter

MAKES 3/4 CUP

This butter is rich in protein and vitamin C.

2 cups water
1 cup rose hips
1/4 cup nut butter
1/2 cup honey

Place the water in a pan and bring to a boil. Add the rose hips; reduce
heat, cover, and simmer for 20 minutes. Drain off the water, then place
the rose hips, nut butter, and honey in a blender; whirl at low speed
until smooth. Use as a jam on toast, biscuits or cookies.

Rose Hip Purée

MAKES 2 CUPS

4 cups water
1 pound rose hips
1 cup honey
Juice of 1 lemon

Bring the water to a boil in a saucepan. Add the rose hips, reduce heat,
cover, and simmer for 20 minutes. Drain off the water, and pour the rose
hips into a ceramic, earthenware, or glass pot. Stir in the honey and
lemon juice; cover, and allow to stand for 24 hours. Pour the purée into
sterilized jars and store in a cool, dark place until ready to use. Use as a
jam on toast, biscuits, or cookies.

Spreads, Toppings, Dips and Snacks **143**

Turkish Honey Gul Surubu (Rose Jam)

MAKES 1 1/4 QUARTS

1 pound rose petals
4 cups honey
Juice of 3 lemons

Gather rose petals that are free from insects and wash them well. Place the rose petals, 2 cups of the honey, and the lemon juice in a large ceramic jar; allow the mixture to stand for 6 days at room temperature.

Then place the remaining 2 cups of honey in a saucepan and bring to a boil; reduce heat and simmer for 10 minutes. Gradually add the petal mixture, stirring gently for 2 minutes with a wooden spoon. Strain the liquid through a fine-meshed strainer, pour into sterilized jars, and cover. Store in a cool place.

Honey Quince Preserve

MAKES 1 1/2 QUARTS

Approximately 3 cups honey
1 1/2 pounds quince, peeled and cored
2 1/2 cups water
Juice of 1 lemon

Cut the quince into small cubes and place in a large saucepan. Cover with cold water and boil for 30 minutes or until tender; drain the quince, reserving the juice. Measure out a cup of honey for each cup of pulp obtained. In a large pan, combine the honey and quince juice and boil for 5 minutes; add the pulp and continue boiling until the fruit is deep red. Pour into sterilized jars and seal.

Fresh Fruit Preserves

Select ripe fruit such as cherries, apricot, prunes, or red currents. Remove the stems and wash carefully. Spread on a cloth to dry. Place the fruit in jars and fill with liquid honey until the fruit is completely covered. Seal with air-tight lids and store in a cool place. These preserves will keep for months.

Honey Nectar Spread

MAKES 1 2/3 CUPS

1 cup fresh pitted apricots
1 cup honey

Combine the ingredients in a blender and blend at low speed to a creamy pulp. Spread on toast, pancakes, breads.
Variation: Honey nectar can be made also with fresh peaches, pineapple chunks, or bananas.

Honey Lemon Butter

MAKES 3/4 CUP

1/2 cup sesame or peanut butter
1/2 cup clover honey
2 tablespoons fresh lemon juice
1 tablespoon grated lemon peel

Place the nut butter in a mixing bowl and beat with a whisk until light and fluffy. Gradually add the honey in a fine stream, beating with the whisk until blended; stir in the lemon juice and lemon peel. Refrigerate at least one hour before serving.

Serve as a dip or spread.

Sweet Pepper Spread

MAKES 1 CUP

1/4 cup honey
1/4 cup lemon juice
1/2 cup tahini
1 green onion, minced
1 small green pepper, minced

Place the ingredients in a blender at low speed for 1 minute. Serve as a condiment with brown rice or as a relish with fowl.

West Indian Honey Gulakund (Rose Jam)   MAKES 1 QUART

1/2 pound rose petals
4 cups light, mild honey (such as honey-
   locust honey)

Wash and dry the petals. Pour 1/4 inch of honey into the bottom of a large earthenware jar. Place a layer of petals on top of the honey. Continue to alternate layers of honey and petals. Close the jar with a tight lid (preferably cork) and place in the sunshine for one week. Serve on toast, bread, or muffins.

Honey Coconut Spread or Dip   MAKES 1 1/4 CUPS

1 cup shredded coconut
1 cup mild flavored honey
2 tablespoons peanut butter

Preheat oven to 350°. Spread the coconut on an ungreased cookie sheet and place in the oven for 6 to 7 minutes until lightly browned. Stir the coconut every 2 minutes so it will toast evenly. Combine the honey and peanut butter in a blender at low speed until smooth; pour into a serving bowl and add the toasted coconut, mixing with a fork. Serve on pancakes, or use as a dip with Natural Potato Chips.

Peanut Pimento Spread or Dip

MAKES 1/2 CUP

2 sweet red peppers, thinly sliced and chopped
1/2 cup peanut butter
2 tablespoons honey
A dash of Tabasco
1 tablespoon pine nuts

Combine the first 4 ingredients in a blender at high speed until smooth. Pour into a bowl and decorate with the pine nuts. Serve as a dip with Natural Potato Chips or spread over a slice of honey bread.

Honey Almond Cream Dip

MAKES 2 CUPS

1 cup cottage cheese
1/2 cup almonds, chopped
1/4 cup honey
1/4 cup fresh orange juice
1/2 an orange cut in wedges
1 tablespoon toasted almonds

Place the first four ingredients in a blender and blend at high speed until smooth. If the mixture is too thick, add a little more orange juice. Pour into a serving bowl and decorate with the orange wedges and toasted almonds. Refrigerate at least one hour before serving.
Variation: Decorate with sunflower seeds or walnuts instead of almonds.

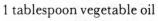

Wild Honey Dip

> 1 tablespoon vegetable oil
> 1 cup grated Swiss cheese
> 1/4 cup wild honey
> 1/2 cup shelled pistachio nuts (or peanuts), chopped
> 1/2 teaspoon saffron
> 1 red chili pepper, minced (to taste)
> Sea salt to taste
> 1 tablespoon shelled pistachio nuts

Coat a saucepan with the oil and place over low heat; add the cheese to the saucepan, slowly stirring with a flat wooden spatula until the cheese threads. Add the next 5 ingredients stirring constantly; continue cooking for 1 to 2 minutes more, or until the ingredients are well blended. Remove from heat and pour into a serving bowl. Decorate with pistachio nuts, and serve immediately.

Snacks

Honey Toast

Toast slices of bread, spread with Honey Butter, and sprinkle with chopped nuts. Place under the broiler for 5 minutes or until the nuts are slightly browned. Serve hot.

Honey Butter Strips

Cut strips of whole wheat bread; spread with a Honey Butter or a Honey Spread and roll in sesame seeds. Toast in a hot oven for 8 minutes or until crisp and brown.

Honey Orange Toast

Spread slices of bread with a Honey Butter or a Honey Spread. Add grated orange rind and chopped nuts. Broil for 5 minutes or until bubbly.

Dry Roasted Nuts and Seeds

Heat a heavy skillet until a sprinkle of water dropped into it will evaporate instantly. Spread seeds or nuts in the skillet and reduce to low heat. Shake the skillet over the burner and stir the seeds or nuts occasionally. Roast seeds for 3 to 4 minutes, and nuts for 10 to 12 minutes until lightly browned. Allow the nuts or seeds to cool, then place in an airtight container and store in a cool, dry place.

Blanched Almonds and Peanuts

Shell the nuts. Bring water to a boil in a saucepan; add the nuts and turn off the heat. Allow the nuts to stand 3 to 4 minutes, then drain off the water. Peel the skins off the nuts with your fingers; do not use a metallic knife. Dry the nuts between two sheets of absorbent paper.

Smoker

Simple Extractor

Straight Knife

Tapered Knife

Spatula

No truly, unless thou wert hard-favoured: for honesty coupled to beauty, is to have honey a sauce to sugar.
—Shakespeare, *As You Like It*

Curved Knife

Wax Knife

Candies and Candied Fruit

Hive with handle for retreiving a Swarm

Spatula

Curved Knife

Wax Knife

Hive with handle for retreiving a Swarm

Fruit Powders for Coating

Save the rinds of oranges, lemons, and tangerines. Hang them on a thread and allow them to dry. When they are thoroughly dried, crush them in a blender at high speed and store in tightly covered jars.

Nougat

MAKES 3 DOZEN

This is one of thirteen traditional desserts served on Christmas day in Provence, France.

4 cups mild honey (clover or orange blossom)
4 cups almonds, shelled
2 to 4 sheets of wafers (according to size)

Pour the honey into a large copper pot; slowly bring to a boil, stirring constantly. As the honey begins to bubble, gradually add the almonds, continuing to stir. When the honey turns brown, dip the spoon covered with honey into a bowl of cold water. Roll a drop of syrup from the spoon into a bead between your fingers; if the bead becomes hard as it cools, the syrup is ready (250° on a candy thermometer). Remove the syrup from heat and continue to stir for approximately 4 minutes.

Line the bottom of a 2 x 8 x 12-inch baking pan with a sheet of paper thin wafer. Pour the syrup on top of the wafer and cover with another sheet of wafer. Lay a wooden board over the nougat; place a 1 pound weight on the board, and press for 15 minutes. Allow the nougat to cool, then slice into strips 1 1/2 inches wide. To store for several months, wrap in pieces of cellophane or waxed paper and place in a covered container.

Honey Pebbles

MAKES 200 PIECES

2 cups honey
5 cups almonds, shelled (or a nut of your choice)

Pour the honey into a large copper pot; bring to a boil, then reduce heat to obtain a medium boil, stirring constantly. When the honey turns light brown and becomes a thick syrup, dip the spoon covered with honey into a bowl of cold water. Take a drop of syrup from the spoon between your fingers, rolling it into a small bead; if the bead becomes hard as it cools, the syrup is ready (275° on a candy thermometer). Turn off the heat.

Drop almonds into the syrup, stirring to coat well. Remove the almonds with a flat skimmer and place on a greased cookie sheet to cool; keep the almonds separated. Repeat the process with the remaining almonds. To obtain a thick coating, dip the almonds in the syrup more than once, allowing them to cool between dips.

Honey Mounds

MAKES 3 DOZEN

1/3 cup butter
1 egg
1/3 cup honey
1 teaspoon vanilla
2 2/3 cups unbleached white flour
1 teaspoon baking soda
1/2 teaspoon sea salt

Combine the butter, egg, and honey in a large bowl; cream well, then add the vanilla. Sift together the flour, soda, and salt and gradually add to the creamed ingredients. Refrigerate the mixture for 1 hour.

Preheat oven to 350°. Place the mixture on a floured board and using the palms of the hands, roll into 1-inch balls. Place on a greased baking sheet; bake for 10 to 15 minutes, or until crisp.

Nut Seed Squares

MAKES 2 DOZEN

1/2 cup coconut, shredded
1/2 cup sunflower seeds, shelled
1/2 cup cashew nuts, chopped
1/2 cup sesame seeds
1/4 cup water
1/2 cup nut butter
1/4 cup honey
1/2 cup powdered milk
1/2 cup raw wheat germ

Combine the first 4 ingredients in a blender and chop. Add water and blend at medium speed until the mixture is paste-like; add the remaining ingredients and blend until smooth. Pour the mixture into an oiled ice cube tray and place in the refrigerator (do not freeze) for about 3 hours. The squares will be semi-soft; pop them out of the tray as you would ice cubes. Store in an air-tight jar.

Honey Fig Squares

MAKES 2 DOZEN

3 eggs
1 cup honey
1 cup unbleached white flour
1 teaspoon baking soda
A dash of sea salt
1 cup chopped nuts (hickory nuts or pine nuts)
1 cup dried figs (diced)

Preheat oven to 325°. Separate the eggs, placing the yolks in one bowl and the whites in another. Add the honey to the yolks and blend well. Sift together the flour, baking soda, and salt, and gradually add to the yolk and honey mixture. Beat the whites until stiff peaks form then carefully fold into the mixture until no large areas of white remain; fold in the nuts and figs. Pour the batter into an oiled 9 x 13-inch pan and bake for 45 minutes. Cool and cut into squares.

For a delicious snack, insert a honey fig square inside a dry fig that is not quite split in two.

Candies and Candied Fruit 153

Pecan Balls

MAKES 6 DOZEN

  1/2 cup sesame butter
  4 tablespoons vegetable oil
  1/2 cup honey
  2 cups sifted unbleached white flour
  1/2 teaspoon sea salt
  2 cups pecans, finely chopped
  Orange rind powder

Preheat oven to 300°. Combine the sesame butter, oil, and honey in a bowl. Sift the flour and salt together and gradually stir into the honey and butter, mixing well; add the chopped nuts.

Form the dough into 1/2-inch balls by rolling between the palms of the hands; place on an oiled cookie sheet and bake for 45 minutes. Remove from the oven, and while still hot, roll the balls in orange rind powder. Allow to cool, and roll again in orange rind powder before serving.

Honey Peanut Rolls

MAKES 2 DOZEN

  1 cup powdered (dry) milk
  1 cup peanut butter (or any Nut Butter)
  1 cup honey
  1/2 teaspoon vanilla
  1/4 cup peanuts, powdered in a blender

Combine the first 4 ingredients in a bowl and mix thoroughly. Shape the dough into 1 1/2-inch-long rolls and coat evenly with the peanut flour.

Honey Hermits

2 cups unbleached white flour
1 teaspoon baking soda
1/2 teaspoon allspice
A dash of sea salt
1/2 cup oil (sesame or corn)
1 cup honey
2 eggs
1/4 cup water
2 cups raisins
1 cup dates, chopped
1/2 cup nuts, chopped

Preheat oven to 375°. Sift the first 4 ingredients into a large mixing bowl. Add the oil, stirring with a wooden spoon or spatula. Gradually add the honey, eggs, and water, stirring slowly and continuously. Fold in the fruit and nuts and continue mixing for 8 to 10 minutes or until the batter is smooth.

Grease two cookie sheets; drop teaspoonfuls of batter onto the cookie sheets, leaving 1-inch space between each. Bake for 12 to 15 minutes.

Honey Caramels

2 1/4 cups dark honey
1/4 cup nut butter
1/4 cup dry milk

Combine all the ingredients in a saucepan and place over low heat, simmering until candy reaches the hard ball stage. Test by dipping spoon covered with syrup into a bowl of cold water. Take a drop of syrup from the spoon between your fingers, rolling it into a small bead; if the bead becomes hard as it cools, the syrup is ready (265° on a candy thermometer).

Remove from the stove and beat 5 to 10 minutes or until syrup is thick. Pour syrup into a wooden candy frame or a greased, 1-inch-high cookie pan. Allow to cool and cut into squares.

Honey Raisin Squares

MAKES 2 DOZEN

1/4 cup sesame oil
1 cup honey
1 egg
1 1/2 cups rolled oats
1 1/2 cups whole wheat pastry flour
1 1/2 teaspoons baking powder
1 cup milk
1/2 teaspoon sea salt
1 cup raisins

Preheat oven to 350°. Combine the oil and honey in a mixing bowl; add the egg and blend well. Add the next 5 ingredients and mix thoroughly; stir in the raisins. Pour the batter into an oiled 2 x 8 x 12-inch pan and bake for 15 to 20 minutes. Cool, and cut into 2-inch squares.
Variation: Substitute the raisins with prunes, dates, figs, or dried apricots.

Honey Orange Crisps

MAKES 2 DOZEN

1 cup honey
3/4 cup peanut oil
1 teaspoon powdered ginger
2 tablespoons fresh orange juice
3 cups unbleached white flour

Combine the oil and honey in a mixing bowl; add the ginger and orange juice, blending until creamy. Gradually add the flour, mixing well. Chill the mixture in the refrigerator for 30 minutes.

Preheat oven to 350°. Turn the dough onto a floured board and roll until 1/2-inch thick; cut into 2-inch squares. Place squares on a greased cookie sheet and bake for 10 minutes.

Honey Carob Fudge

MAKES 3 DOZEN

2 tablespoons carob powder
2/3 cup nut butter
2 eggs
1 cup honey
1 teaspoon vanilla
1 cup unbleached white flour, sifted
1/2 teaspoon sea salt
1 teaspoon baking soda
1/2 cup walnuts, chopped

Preheat oven to 350°. Melt the carob powder and nut butter in a double boiler over high heat; remove from heat and allow to cool. Beat the eggs until fluffy and add to the carob mixture. Gradually add the remaining ingredients; mix until thoroughly blended. Pour the batter into a greased 2 x 8 x 12-inch baking pan; bake for 25 minutes. Cool, then cut into 1-inch squares.

Candied Apricots

MAKES 3 DOZEN

4 cups honey
4 cups apricots, dried and halved

Bring the honey to a boil in a deep pot, stirring with a wooden spoon; reduce heat and simmer until the honey forms a thick brown syrup. Dip the spoon covered with honey into a bowl of cold water; the syrup on the spoon will crack if it is ready (300° on a candy thermometer).

Place 4 or 5 apricot halves on a skewer and dip the skewer into the gently bubbling syrup. With the flat side of a knife, or with a fork, slide the apricots off the skewer onto a greased cookie sheet to cool. Repeat the process several times with each batch of apricots to obtain a thick coating.

Variation: Fruits such as apples, bananas, sliced pears, orange wedges, pineapple chunks, tangerine wedges, kumquats, and melon chunks can also be candied using the same procedure as above.

Spatula

Curved Knife

Wax Knife

Hive with handle for retreiving a Swarm

Marrons Glacés (Candied Chestnuts)

MAKES 4 DOZEN

"Marrons glacés" are traditionally given as gifts in France on New Year's Day.

2 pounds chestnuts
4 cups honey

Preheat the oven to 350°. Slit the shell of each chestnut and place on a cookie sheet; roast until the shells loosen (about 30 minutes). Allow the chestnuts to cool, then peel off the shells and skins.

Bring the honey to a boil in a deep pot; reduce heat and simmer, stirring constantly with a wooden spoon. When the honey syrup is light brown, dip the spoon covered with honey into a bowl of cold water; if the syrup on the spoon becomes hard enough to crack (300° on a candy thermometer), it is ready.

Carefully place a few roasted chestnuts on a skimmer and dip them into the bubbling syrup: coat well, then place the glazed chestnuts on a greased cookie sheet to cool. Store in a sterilized, airtight jar.

Your promise, how sweet to my palate!
Sweeter than honey to my mouth!
—Psalms 119

Spatula

Curved
Knife

Wax
Knife

Beverages

Hive with
handle
for
retreiving
a
Swarm

Eggnog

MAKES 3 CUPS

4 eggs
4 tablespoons honey
3 cups milk
1 teaspoon vanilla
A dash of nutmeg
A dash of sea salt

Separate the eggs, and beat the whites until stiff. Blend in the yolks, then add the remaining ingredients, mixing until smooth. Delicious served hot (do not boil) or cold.

Strawberry Cooler

MAKES 1 GALLON

1 pint fresh strawberries, sliced
1/2 cup honey
6 ounces frozen orange juice concentrate
1 cup pineapple juice
1 quart milk
1 pint pineapple sherbet

Combine the strawberries and the honey in a blender at high speed; add the orange juice concentrate, pineapple juice and milk, blending until smooth. Pour the mixture into tall, chilled glasses and top with a scoop of sherbet.

Banana Shake

MAKES 3 CUPS

2 cups chilled milk
1/2 cup chilled orange juice
2 tablespoons honey
1 banana, peeled and sliced
1/4 cup prune juice

Combine all the ingredients in a blender and blend at high speed until smooth.

Grapefruit Tea Cooler

MAKES 12 CUPS

8 tea bags
2 cups water
1 cup honey
2 quarts ice water
1/2 cup lime juice
2 6-ounce cans frozen concentrated grape-
    fruit juice, thawed and undiluted

Place the tea bags in a large bowl or tall pitcher. Bring the water to a boil; pour over the tea bags and allow them to steep for 5 minutes. Remove the tea bags and add honey, stirring until dissolved. Add the remaining ingredients and blend thoroughly. Serve over crushed ice in tall glasses.

Honey Passion

MAKES 4 CUPS

2 bananas, peeled and sliced
2 cups orange juice
1 teaspoon honey
2 cups pineapple juice
8 large strawberries

Combine all ingredients in a blender and blend until smooth. Chill before serving.

Honey Lemon Drink

MAKES 4 CUPS

1 tablespoon freshly grated lemon peel
1 cup honey
1 cup boiling water
1 1/2 cups freshly squeezed lemon juice

Combine the lemon peel, honey, and boiling water in a pitcher; add the lemon juice and blend. Store in the refrigerator until ready to use. Serve over crushed ice.

Honey Zabaglione (Italian Eggnog)

SERVES 3 TO 4

    4 egg yolks
    3 tablespoons honey
    1 cup sherry
    A dash of cinnamon

Combine the egg yolks and honey in the top of a double boiler and beat the mixture until thick. Place over high heat and gradually add the sherry, beating until smooth. Sprinkle with cinnamon. Serve hot or cold.

Honey Krambambuli (Punch)

MAKES 1 QUART

    1 quart dry white wine
    1/4 cup orange juice
    1 tablespoon lemon juice
    1 stick cinnamon
    1 lemon, quartered
    1 orange, quartered
    2 cloves
    1/3 cup rum
    1/4 cup honey

Combine the first seven ingredients in a large pan; bring to a simmer over medium heat; reduce heat if necessary and continue to simmer for 8 minutes. Strain into a punch bowl.

Pour the honey into an earthenware bowl. Place the rum in a ladle and light the rum with a long match; pour over the honey, which will caramelize lightly. Add to the wine mixture, and mix with the ladle.

Honey Cider

MAKES 1 QUART

1 quart apple cider
1/4 cup honey
6 sticks of cinnamon
12 cloves
A dash of sea salt

Bring the apple cider to a boil in a saucepan. Add the remaining ingredients and return to a boil for 3 minutes. Remove the pan from the heat and allow the mixture to stand overnight to develop flavor. Strain the cider through a fine mesh strainer, removing the cinnamon and cloves. Serve chilled over Honey Ice Cubes.

Honey Berry Wine

MAKES 2 GALLONS

2 gallons of any kind of fresh, very ripe berries
2 gallons of soft water or rain water
6 to 8 pounds of honey

Wash and dry the berries carefully. Place them in an earthenware crock and add 2 gallons of boiling, soft water. Allow to cool, then mash the berries with a wooden pestle. Cover the crock with a piece of muslin and place in a warm area (70°–80°) for 5 days or until a crust forms; then strain through a muslin cloth into another earthenware crock.

Measure the liquid after straining; add 4 pounds of honey for each gallon of liquid. Cover with muslin, and allow to ferment again for 10 days. Then place a large lid on top of the muslin covered crock, making sure no air can penetrate. Allow the mixture to stand for at least 6 months.

With a rubber tube, siphon the wine into sterilized glass bottles, cork tightly, and place the bottles in a dark, cool place, allowing the wine to rest for about 2 months before using. The wine will keep for years.

Hydromel

MAKES 6 GALLONS

Use any honey of your choice. The kind of honey used will dictate the specific taste of the hydromel.

    6 gallons of soft water (or rain water)
    15 pounds of raw honey
    1 1/2 cakes dry active yeast

Combine the water and the honey in an extra large kettle. Bring to a boil, reduce heat, and allow to boil gently, skimming the foam constantly for about 2 hours. When the surface is completely clear, remove from heat and allow the mixture to cool.

Pour or draw the mixture into a large, clean wooden barrel; add the yeast, cover the bung-hole with muslin or gauze to keep out insects, and place the barrel in a warm area (70°–80°). Allow the mixture to ferment for about 2 weeks.

Foam will escape from the bung and should be skimmed off each day, but keep the level constant by adding honey and water mixed in equal proportions. When the fermentation process is completed and foam ceases to form (about 2 weeks), close the bung with a cork, and allow to stand for 1 month before bottling.

Siphon the liquid into sterilized, glass bottles, cork the bottles, and store in a dark cool place for 1 month before using.

Metheglin (Old English mead recipe)

MAKES 2 GALLONS

    12 quarts of rain water
    2 quarts honey
    1 tablespoon ginger
    1 cake dry active yeast

Combine the water, honey and ginger in an extra large kettle. Bring to a boil, reduce to medium, and boil until 1/3 of the liquid evaporates. Turn off heat and allow to cool. Pour the mixture into a large earthenware jar and add the yeast. Allow to stand for 3 days.

With a yard of rubber or plastic tube, siphon the liquid into sterilized, glass bottles. Cork, and place the bottles in a cool dark place; allow to stand 3 weeks before using.

Honey Sangria

MAKES 6 CUPS

1 bottle (4/5 qt.) Burgundy
3 tablespoons apricot brandy
1 cup orange juice
1 lemon, unpeeled and thinly sliced
1/2 cup fresh lemon juice
1/4 cup honey
1 orange, peeled and thinly sliced
1 lime, unpeeled and thinly sliced
2 fresh peaches, peeled and thinly sliced
1 apple, diced
1/2 cup strawberries, sliced
1 bottle (7 oz.) club soda, chilled

Combine all the ingredients except the club soda in a serving bowl; blend well and chill. Add the club soda just before serving.

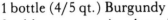

Honey Ice Cubes

MAKES 12 CUBES

1/2 cup honey
2 cups very hot water
2 tablespoons fresh lemon juice

Combine the ingredients in a bowl, mixing well. Pour into ice cube trays and place in the freezer. Serve in iced tea or fruit punch.

Recipe Index

Medicinal and Cosmetic Index